SPLENDID
SAMPLERS
to Cross-Stitch

$\mathscr{S}$PLENDID SAMPLERS
to Cross-Stitch
35 Original Projects

Chris Rankin

Sterling Publishing Co., Inc.   New York
A STERLING/LARK BOOK

Editor: Bobbe Needham
Art Director: Chris Bryant
Production: Elaine Thompson
English Translation: Networks, Inc., and Irene Selent
Editorial Assistance: Stephanie Johnston and Ethan Skemp

Library of Congress Cataloging-in-Publication Data
Rankin, Chris.
    Splendid samplers to cross-stitch : 35 original projects / Chris Rankin.
      p.   cm.
    "A Sterling/Lark book."
    Includes index.
    ISBN 0-8069-3164-7
    1. Needlework--Patterns.   2. Samplers.   I. Title.
TT753.R36   1995
746.44'2041--dc20   95-11548
                                            CIP

A Sterling/Lark Book

Produced by Altamont Press, Inc.
  50 College St., Asheville, NC 28801

Published in 1995 by Sterling Publishing Co., Inc.
  387 Park Ave. South, New York, NY 10016

Pages 46, 47, 56, 92–93: Photos and original instructions
© Libelle Special/Uitgeverij Spaarnestad, Haarlem, Holland

Other project photos and original instructions
© Ariadne/Spaarnestad, Utrecht, Holland
English translation © 1995, Altamont Press

Distributed in Canada by Sterling Publishing,
  c/o Canadian Manda Group, One Atlantic Avenue, Suite 105,
  Toronto, Ontario, Canada M6K 3E7

Distributed in Great Britain and Europe by Cassell PLC,
  Wellington House, 125 Strand, London WC2R 0BB, England

Distributed in Australia by Capricorn Link (Australia) Pty Ltd.
  P.O. Box 6651, Baulkham Hills, Business Centre,
  NSW 2153, Australia

ISBN 0-8069-3164-7

Contents

Introduction

WHAT IS IT ABOUT SAMPLERS? I've always been drawn to them. Hanging in antique stores, on a friend's wall, or in a historic home, those pictures painted with thread, those mottos and alphabets, names and dates written with tiny stitches speak to me of time and care and artistry.

Maybe it's the history. Maybe it's knowing that children and women (mostly) have been stitching samplers for centuries. Maybe it's imagining ten-year-old girls sitting in a row in a schoolroom in seventeenth-century England or eighteenth-century Connecticut, poking their needles in and out of somewhat grimy, unevenly woven linen under a schoolmistress's watchful eye.

Twelve-year-old Elizabeth Boulton stitched this sampler in silk on wool in early nineteenth-century England. Reproduced with permission, Division of Textiles, National Museum of American History, Smithsonian Institution.

WHAT WAS PARADISE
BUT A GARDEN
AN ORCHARD
OF TREES AND HERBS
FULL OF PLEASURE, AND
NOTHING THERE BUT
DELIGHTS'
WILLIAM LAWSON

Directions for this project begin on page 118.

OR MAYBE IT'S THE NEEDLEWORKERS I KNOW TODAY—Stephanie, a college chemistry major, who creates her own beautiful designs; two friends I overheard in a crafts shop exclaiming over the sampler patterns like kids in a toy store; my father stitching nautical scenes as he watched the sun set from the kitchen of his Bahamas cottage.

Whatever it is about samplers, it respects no borders—people of all nationalities, ages, genders, and religions have enjoyed stitching samplers and taken pleasure in looking at them for centuries. To retain a bit of this history, I introduce the samplers in the book with quotations, most from early American samplers. (I've printed them as they were stitched, misspellings and all, because I feel these make them unique and human.)

Whichever samplers you choose to work, I believe that with each line of stitching you gift the world with your own artistry and add your own unique threads to the ongoing tapestry of needlework.

Starting Out

HERE'S the secret to a beautiful cross-stitched sampler: work all the upper crossing stitches in the same direction—say, from the lower left to the upper right of the x. Crossing the stitches in different directions makes the light reflect off them differently and makes them look uneven. Break this rule to emphasize a part of the design—switch the direction of your upper stitches in that area.

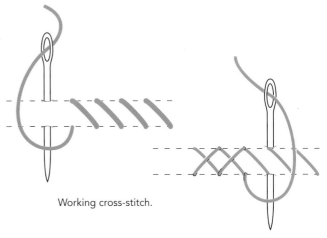

Working cross-stitch.

To save time and thread, work back and forth across a motif in rows, slanting all the lower threads one way as you stitch in one direction and the upper threads the other way on the return trip, as shown in the two illustrations.

For diagonal rows of stitches, scattered individual stitches, or single stitches of one color, most cross-stitchers find that completing one stitch at a time works best.

Deciding on Fabrics

TO WORK a sampler, you have to be able to count the threads of your fabric, because you make each cross-stitch over an intersection of those threads. Typical project directions in the book, for example, tell you to "cross-stitch the motif using two strands of floss over two threads" of fabric for each stitch.

Today's even-weave fabrics, with the same number of warp and weft threads per inch or per centimeter, help ensure you even cross-stitches. Although any even-weave fabric will work, one that a veteran cross-stitcher finds challenging and satisfying might discourage a beginner. Close weaves—that is, those with more threads to the inch—mean more difficult and exacting needlework. The paragraph on materials for each project tells you what fabric appears in the pictured example, including its thread count—for instance, "ecru linen with 25 threads per inch (10 per cm)."

The samplers in the book call for popular and easy-to-find even-weave fabrics: linen, Aida, and Hardanger. Probably the most expensive of these, linen is both beautiful and durable and comes in weaves from coarse to fine. Two popular cottons are Aida cloth, which is 100 percent cotton and has between eleven and twenty-two threads per inch, and Hardanger cloth, a cotton blend that resists fraying, with twenty-five or twenty-seven threads to the inch.

Using the Charts

EACH sampler in the book has an accompanying chart—a graph of the finished embroidery. Each symbol on the chart represents one cross-stitch, and the key to the chart lists a different color of floss for each symbol.

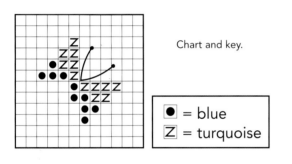

Chart and key.

● = blue
Z = turquoise

On the chart for the butterfly shown here, for instance, the dots stand for blue and the z's for turquoise. To stitch the butterfly, on the bottom row you make one blue stitch; on the second row, another blue stitch above it and one to the right; on the third row, working from left to right, two blue stitches, then two turquoise stitches, and so on.

To keep your place on the chart, you might move a small ruler or index card down the rows as you work or pencil through each row as you complete it.

Before you begin a sampler, you'll want to be sure your finished embroidery will end up in the middle of the fabric. Matching the center of the motif (that is, the center of the chart) to the center of your fabric ensures that your embroidery won't run off one side. To find the center of the fabric, fold the fabric end to end, then side to side. Mark both centerlines with tailor's chalk, straight pins, or basting thread.

You can then count the stitches on the chart from this central point to each edge, translate this figure onto your fabric in terms of threads per stitch, and figure out where the edges of your embroidery will fall. Say you

count 100 stitches (squares) on the chart from the center to the right-hand edge, and the directions call for making each stitch over two threads of fabric. You can figure the right-hand edge of your embroidery will fall 200 threads to the right of the centerline on your fabric.

Selecting Needles, Floss, and Hoops

THE LARGE eyes and blunt points of tapestry needles make them ideal for cross-stitching, for they hold multiple strands of floss and push the fabric fibers apart without splitting threads or previous stitches. A packet of assorted sizes (say, #20 to #24) will work for most fabrics. The higher the number, the smaller the needle. Coarser fabrics call for larger needles, finer fabrics for smaller. For example, a #24 needle works well for eleven-count Aida cloth—that is, for any fabric with eleven threads per inch (4.5 per cm).

The six-strand cotton embroidery floss cross-stitchers use comes in almost every conceivable color. Each skein runs approximately nine yards (8.2 m). For each sampler in the book, the key to the chart supplies, along with each color, the corresponding product number for two widely available brands of floss, DMC and Anchor. (You may of course substitute another brand—or even rewrite the color key.) When the pictured samplers have been worked in some other thread, that is noted and its color numbers listed.

Many cross-stitchers find that embroidery hoops slow them down or distort stitches, and leaving work in a hoop even overnight may permanently stretch the fabric. Ironing the finished sampler takes care of any fabric creases or unevenness of tension in the stitches. If you feel that a hoop helps keep your stitching even, look for a two-ring wood or plastic hoop that you can adjust with a screw on the outer ring.

Sampler Tip
BLEEDING FLOSS

If you're unsure whether a particular color of floss will bleed (that is, whether the color will run), wash the skein in plenty of lukewarm water. If it bleeds, rinse it with cold water until the water runs clear. Don't wring it out. Fold it in a towel and press out the moisture, then let it dry.

Making a Floss Caddy

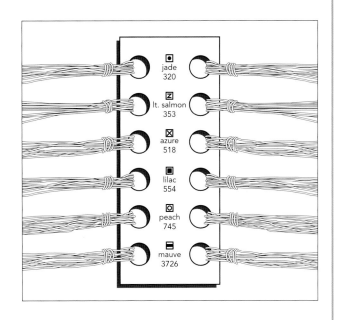

ESPECIALLY when your project calls for many colors of floss, you may yearn for a way to organize all those skeins. Craft or fabric shops offer a variety of organizers, but you can easily make one, as shown here.

Punch holes along the sides of a stiff card or piece of cardboard. Then cut one skein of the floss called for in your project to lengths of about fourteen to twenty-four inches (36 to 62 cm) each. Hold one end of the lengths together and thread this through a hole in the cardboard, as shown here. Label each skein with its symbol on the key to the project chart, its brand, and its shade number.

Working Cross-Stitch

A SHORT length of floss works best for cross-stitching—about fourteen to twenty-four inches (36 to 62 cm).

~ THE FABRIC ~

To keep your fabric from fraying as you work at your embroidery, you need to finish the raw edges in one of several ways. For closely woven fabric, you can finish the edges with a row of machine or hand zigzag stitches. For most fabrics, you can simply turn over a narrow hem and stitch it by hand or machine. For canvas, fold masking tape around the edges or fold cotton binding over them and stitch it down firmly.

~ THE FIRST STITCH ~

Especially in looser fabric weaves, you can see that a larger opening occurs between every second thread. To make your stitch counting much easier, make your first stitch next to the vertical thread with the larger opening.

~ NEW THREAD ~

Cross-stitchers use two methods for anchoring the first stitch of a project or of a new area: leaving a tail and looping. In the first method, you leave a one-inch (2.5 cm) tail of floss dangling free at the back, then catch this tail under the next few stitches, as shown in the illustration.

The loop method works anytime you are sewing with an even number of strands of floss (the directions for each sampler specify how many strands of floss to use). For example, if the directions call for two strands of floss, cut one strand that is twice as long as the length you want to stitch with. Fold it in half and thread the needle with the two ends together, leaving a loop at the other end. Come up from the back of your fabric and make the first half cross. When you pass the needle to the back again, run it through the loop before coming up to complete the cross-stitch.

Once your sampler is under way, start new strands by running your needle under a few already worked stitches on the back of the design, then come up on the right side to begin stitching.

Avoid carrying floss across the back of an open area of light fabric for more than five squares. Dark threads especially will show through.

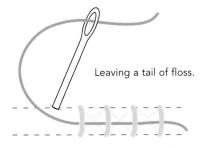

Leaving a tail of floss.

~ COLOR PLAN ~

To conserve floss, plan ahead with colors. For instance, you may stitch a turquoise flower and see that you will need turquoise again in a nearby bud. Rather than clipping off your thread and starting a new one with every color change, after you stitch the flower carry the long remaining turquoise strand along the back of your work to an out-of-the-way spot on the fabric, pull it through to the front, and take the needle off, as shown in the illustration of the vase. Continue stitching the other

Floss color planning.

colors called for in the design. When you reach the turquoise bud, pull the dangling strand through to the back of the work, rethread it, and travel on the wrong side to the bud, weaving through the backs of your newly embroidered stitches.

~ THE LAST STITCH ~

When you finish a color or strand, run the last inch or so of floss under a few stitches on the back of the sampler so no loose end shows. Snip off any excess.

When you're not embroidering, remove your needle (and hoop, if you use one) from the fabric—both leave rust marks.

Using Other Stitches

MOST projects in the book suggest that you embroider around the figures in your finished sampler with an outline stitch; some also call for a smattering of other common embroidery stitches. These are described and pictured in the stitches appendix.

Changing Sizes

TO VARY the finished size of a sampler, make your cross-stitches larger or smaller—that is, cross more or fewer threads with each stitch than the instructions call for. You'll also have to refigure the amount of fabric you'll need.

If you decide to use a different fabric or to design your own project, plan your stitch size based on the effect you want. On a fabric with fewer (thus, thicker) threads per inch, crossing two threads for each stitch gives you good-sized stitches. On a fine-woven fabric that has more threads per inch, crossing two threads results in tiny, fine stitches.

Something else to keep in mind: the more threads of fabric you cross with one stitch, the less solid the mass of color that will result, because more fabric will show behind the stitches. Also, the more strands of floss you use, the thicker and bolder the stitch. In general, stitches look best when they fill the holes of the fabric but still retain the clarity of the cross.

Choosing Colors

WHEN it comes to choosing colors for your sampler, you are the king or queen of the realm. Taste, personal preference, decor, mood, time of day—anything you choose can govern the colors of your cross-stitch project. Each sampler chart in this book comes with a color key that reflects the floss colors used in the pictured projects, but feel free to design your own palette. A color tip: When choosing floss, lay it over the fabric you will use under natural light.

Changing Letters and Numbers

YOU will nearly always want to substitute other names and dates for the ones pictured on the samplers here (except perhaps for the historic samplers). Let's say you want one line of your sampler to read "April 2, 1996," as shown here. On the original project chart:

1. Count across to find the cross-stitches allowed on each line (in this theoretical case, 82 are allowed).

2. Choose an alphabet size and style from another sampler or design your own. Count the number of spaces allowed between each letter in a word (we'll say 2), between each number in a date (2), and between each complete word or date (4).

3. If you want to include commas, periods, or hyphens, count the spaces between a word or date and a mark of punctuation (in this case, 2).

4. To make your own chart on graph paper, first mark the beginning and end points of the spaces allowed on a line of your project. In this example, we have 82 spaces to work with. Divide by two to find the center point on the chart (in this case, 41). Add up the spaces between letters and words (here, they total 24).

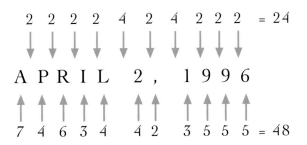

5. Add up the spaces required for each letter and number in your phrase (here, 48). Add this figure to the total of spaces in step 4: 48 + 24 = 72. We have a fit, with 5 squares of space left on each side (82-72=10).

If you find you have too much extra space, you can repeat symbols from elsewhere in the piece. To shrink lines you can abbreviate words, substitute initials for names, and so on.

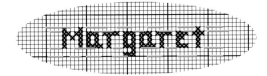

To avoid frustration, use guidelines for names, dates, and borders, as shown in the "Margaret" illustration here:

frame tricky sections of your motif by basting straight lines with bright-colored single strands of floss. When you finish cross-stitching that area, remove the basting.

Antiquing

TO GIVE your sampler an antique look, wet white or ivory linen in plain water, then soak it in strong, cold tea for about ten minutes, stirring occasionally (the fabric will dry a shade lighter). Hot tea will produce a lighter shade, cold coffee a darker one. To set the color so it won't streak if you wash it later, add a teaspoon of alum, available at drugstores. Allow the piece to drip dry, and iron before cross-stitching.

Aging works just as well for a sampler you have already embroidered, as long as the thread is color fast.

Washing and Pressing

IF YOUR finished sampler needs washing and the fabric and floss are washable, launder it like any other delicate item: slosh gently in lukewarm water and mild soap, then rinse. Depending on the fabric, either (1) roll the sampler in a towel to blot up excess moisture, then hang or lay flat to dry, or (2) machine dry it, removing it from the dryer while it is still slightly damp.

To iron out wrinkles and unevenness, cover your ironing board with a towel, then a soft cloth—ironing on a towel helps push the stitches out from the fabric, rather than flattening them down. Place your sampler face down on the cloth and cover it with another soft cloth, dampened if your piece is dry. Press lightly with a fairly hot iron. Lay the sampler flat until it dries completely.

Sampler Tip
FRAMING AND CARE

- Like a lot of us, fabrics prefer to breathe—it lengthens their life. When you frame your sampler or have it framed, try to resist covering it with glass or plastic. Just frame it.

- For storage, wrap your framed sampler in a clean pillowcase (not plastic) and set it at a slight tilt in an airy space.

- Hang your sampler away from direct sunlight, working fireplaces, or crowded kitchens—sunlight will fade it, and soot, smoke, and kitchen grease will discolor it.

Country Garden Sampler

FROM AN 1800S SAMPLER,
WHOSE MAKER LATER REMOVED THE DATE:

*"That which fragrance is to the rose,
modesty is to youth and beauty
Sharpsburg Md 18 —
Eliza Ann Showmans work done
in the 14 year of her age April 22"*

FINISHED MEASUREMENTS

16-1/2 x 22-1/4 in. (42 x 57 cm)

EMBROIDERY MEASUREMENTS

12-3/4 x 19 in. (33 x 49 cm)

MATERIALS

23-1/2 x 29-1/4 in. (60 x 75 cm) of linen with 25 threads per inch (10 per cm); embroidery floss as indicated on the key to the chart plus light topaz #725 or #305; frame (optional).

DIRECTIONS

Mark the horizontal and vertical center of the fabric with basting thread, then cross-stitch according to the chart using two strands of floss over two threads of linen for each stitch.

Embroider in outline stitch over completed cross-stitch using one strand of floss:

- very dark fawn #632 or #936 in and around the tan and medium light copper pots;
- and in and around the remaining pots, the column, the bench, the wheelbarrow, the watering can, and the birds with charcoal #3799 or #236.

Embroider the remaining outline stitches in the same color as the cross-stitches or one shade darker.

Make a French knot at the centers of the flowers where indicated by black circles: in the flowers in the small pot at upper right in light pink #818 or #23; in the flowers in the pot under the arch in light grape #341 or #117; and in the pots to the left and the far right of the column in light topaz #725 or #305.

At the bottom of the sampler, make a French knot at the centers of the tall flowers at the far left in light topaz #725 or #305; in the green flowers in the small pots to the left in grape #340 or #118; and in the pine-colored flowers to the right in a mix of these two colors.

Use two strands of medium light loden green floss #3053 or #261 to embroider the flower stems and the grass next to the pots in stem stitch.

Using three strands and a daisy stitch, embroider the flower petals in the pot left of the column with grape #340 or #118, and the flower petals in the lower left pot with light blue #3755 or #140.

KEY TO CHART

		DMC	Anchor
◣	= gray	318	399
◤	= grape	340	118
⟋	= light grape	341	117
⊘	= turf	371	854
=	= light turf	372	853
H	= tan	437	362
◥	= dark fog	451	233
◖	= pine	502	876
⟋	= light pine	503	875
⧅	= light jade	504	213
⊠	= med. light gray green	523	859
N	= light violet	553	98
L	= lilac	554	96
■	= very dark fawn	632	936
⊓	= medium linen	642	392
•	= very light ecru	712	926
◿	= light tan	738	361
−	= medium light copper	758	882
∴	= silver	762	234
⟋	= light pink	818	23
⊓	= medium glacier blue	827	159
⦂	= denim blue	932	920
∶	= copper	945	881
⊠	= medium light green	987	244
◿	= medium lime	989	242
⟋	= linen	3033	391
◗	= very light turf	3047	852
◢	= medium loden green	3052	262
⊠	= med. light loden green	3053	261
∨	= medium copper	3064	883
◥	= dark loden green	3362	263
▽	= light loden green	3364	260
+	= medium pink	3716	25
⊠	= light blue	3755	140
◉	= charcoal	3799	236

Alphabets in Blue Sampler

FROM A 1630 SAMPLER:

"Caty Langdon is my name
And with my needle I rought the same
And if my skil had been better
I would have mended every letter."

FRAMED MEASUREMENTS

15-1/4 x 18 in. (39 x 46 cm)

EMBROIDERY MEASUREMENTS

12 x 15 in. (31 x 38.5 cm)

MATERIALS

23-1/2 x 25-1/4 in. (60 x 65 cm) of white linen with 26 threads per inch (10 to 11 per cm); embroidery floss as indicated on the key to the chart; a frame 15-1/4 x 18 in. (39 x 46 cm), if desired.

DIRECTIONS

Mark the horizontal and vertical center of the fabric with basting thread, then cross-stitch the motif according to the chart, using two strands of floss over two threads of linen for each stitch.

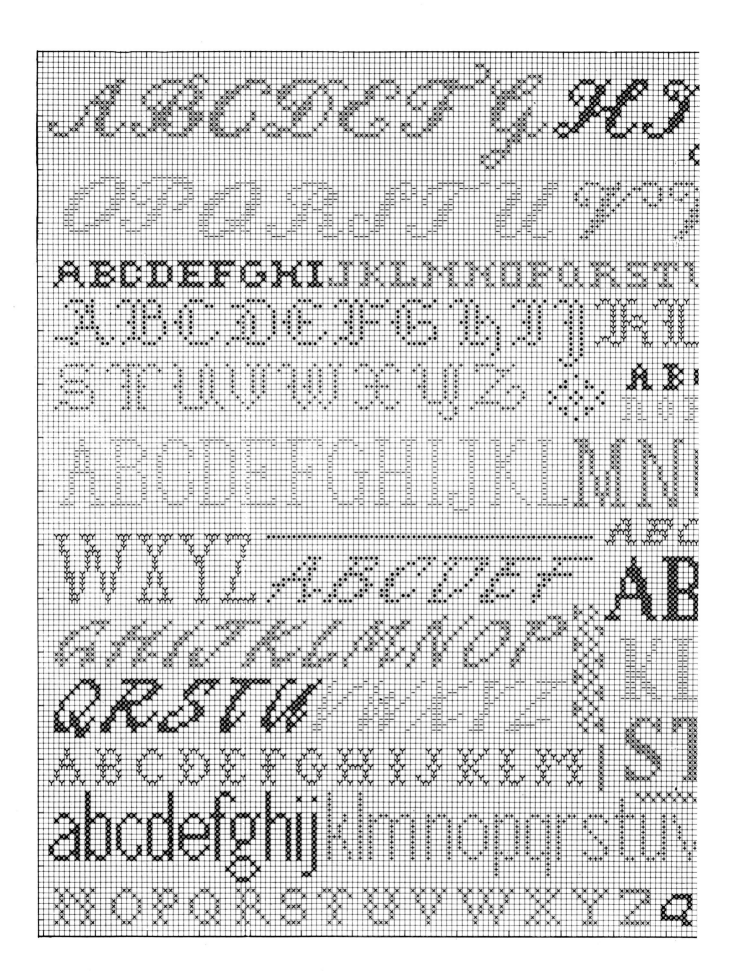

KEY TO CHART

		DMC	Anchor
●	= sapphire	517	162
◉	= navy	796	133
⊠	= dark cobalt	798	131
Y	= medium teal	806	169
−	= medium cobalt	809	130
+	= light sapphire	813	161

Plum Vine Sampler

FROM A 1630 SAMPLER:

"Who was it took such pains
To teach me very plain
With care to mark my name
my Aunt.
John Nichols
Hackleton
Aged 6, 1858"

EMBROIDERY MEASUREMENTS

5-1/2 x 5-1/2 in. (14 x 14 cm)

MATERIALS

A piece of ecru linen 11-3/4 x 11-3/4 in. (30 x 30 cm) with 30 threads per inch (12 per cm); DMC or Anchor embroidery floss as indicated on the key to the chart plus very dark wine #221 or #897; frame (optional).

DIRECTIONS

Mark the horizontal and vertical center of the fabric with basting thread, then cross-stitch the motif according to the chart using two strands of floss over two threads of linen for each stitch.

Embroider the plums in outline stitch over completed cross-stitch using one strand of very dark wine floss #221 or #897.

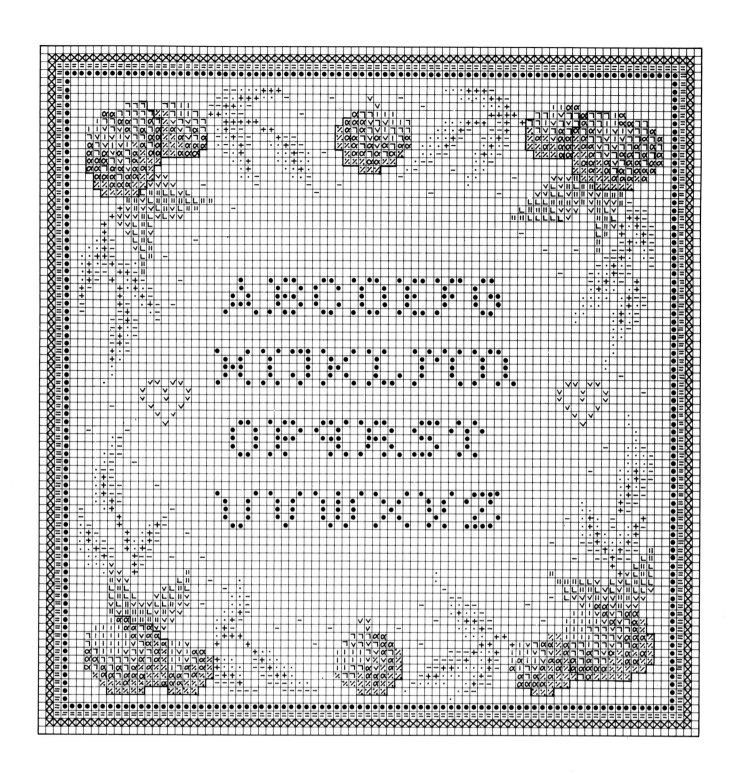

KEY TO CHART

		DMC	Anchor
⋈	= medium wine	223	895
╎	= wine	224	893
⊠	= blue black	336	150
‖	= medium dark pine	501	878
∨	= gray green	522	860

		DMC	Anchor
⌐	= light gray green	524	858
═	= dark sapphire	825	164
●	= sapphire	826	162
+	= dark gray green	926	850
−	= gray green	927	849

		DMC	Anchor
·	= light gray green	928	274
⌐	= blush	3354	74
⦚	= dark wine	3721	896

Christmas Sampler

"The smarting Whip-stitch,
Back-stitch and the Crosse-stitch,
All these are good and we must allow
And these are everywhere in practise now."

—JOHN TAYLOR, "THE PRAISE OF THE NEEDLE," 1631

FINISHED MEASUREMENTS

15-1/2 x 24 in. (39.5 x 61.5 cm)

EMBROIDERY MEASUREMENTS

14-1/4 x 22-1/2 in. (36.5 x 58 cm)

MATERIALS

21-1/2 x 31-1/4 in. (55 x 80 cm) of white linen with 25 threads per inch (10 per cm); embroidery floss as indicated on the key to the chart; a matching frame (optional).

DIRECTIONS

Mark the horizontal and vertical center of the fabric with basting thread, then cross-stitch the motif according to the chart using two strands of floss over two threads of linen for each stitch. *Note: Work the light fawn #3774 or #376 cross-stitch in the hearth using one strand of floss.*

Continue the border around all sides to correspond to the right half.

Embroider in outline stitch over completed cross-stitch using two strands of floss:
- blue black #336 or #150 to outline the Christmas bells, the evergreen branches, the wreath bow, the large Christmas tree, the flame of the candle, the top and the front of the rocking horse's head, and the bows of the packages;
- medium pine #502 or #877 to outline the harness of the rocking horse;
- brick #356 or #5975 to outline the open hearth and the rocking horse;
- very dark fawn #632 or #936 to outline the Santa in the ornament;
- light carmine #815 or #43 for the large stitches of the Christmas stocking;
- and for all remaining outline stitches, medium dark coral #347 or #1025.

Design Note: You might want to embroider the small Christmas motifs separately on Christmas cards, clothing, placecards, or table linen or use them on tree decorations.

KEY TO CHART

		DMC	Anchor
•	= white	white	1
◣	= blue black	336	150
⊠	= medium dark coral	347	1025
⌄	= brick	356	5975

CHRISTMAS SAMPLER

	DMC	Anchor		DMC	Anchor		DMC	Anchor
= dark pine	500	879	= very light pine	504	1042	= light carmine	815	43
= medium dark pine	501	878	= very dark fawn	632	936	= dark salmon	817	13
= medium pine	502	877	= medium light copper	758	882	= medium cocoa	3773	1008
= light pine	503	875	= medium light coral	760	1022	= light fawn	3774	376

Nautical Sampler

FROM A SAMPLER HONORING
GEORGE WASHINGTON'S INAUGURATION:

*" Pitch upon that course of life
which is the most excellent,
and habit will render it the
most delightful…
Mary Varick. 1789. New York."*

FINISHED MEASUREMENTS

17 x 21 in. (43.5 x 54 cm)

EMBROIDERY MEASUREMENTS

15-1/2 x 19-1/2 in. (40 x 50 cm)

MATERIALS

23-1/2 x 27-1/4 in. (60 x 70 cm) of double-thread canvas with 7-1/2 mesh holes per inch (3 per cm); embroidery floss or DMC embroidery cotton as indicated on the key to the chart; (optional) a frame, or a piece of pressboard 17 x 21 in. (43.5 x 54 cm) and a piece of flannel 23-1/2 x 27-1/4 in. (60 x 70 cm).

DIRECTIONS

Mark the horizontal and vertical center of the fabric with basting thread and cross-stitch the motif according to the chart. For both cross-stitches and outline stitches, use one strand of embroidery cotton or six strands of floss over one mesh hole for each stitch.

Replace the word "boudewign" in the lower left of the sampler with the name or boat name of your choice, using letters from either of the alphabets.

Embroider in outline stitch over completed cross-stitch, using the same colors as the cross-stitches.

If you wish, frame your embroidery or cover the pressboard with the flannel and stretch your sampler over it.

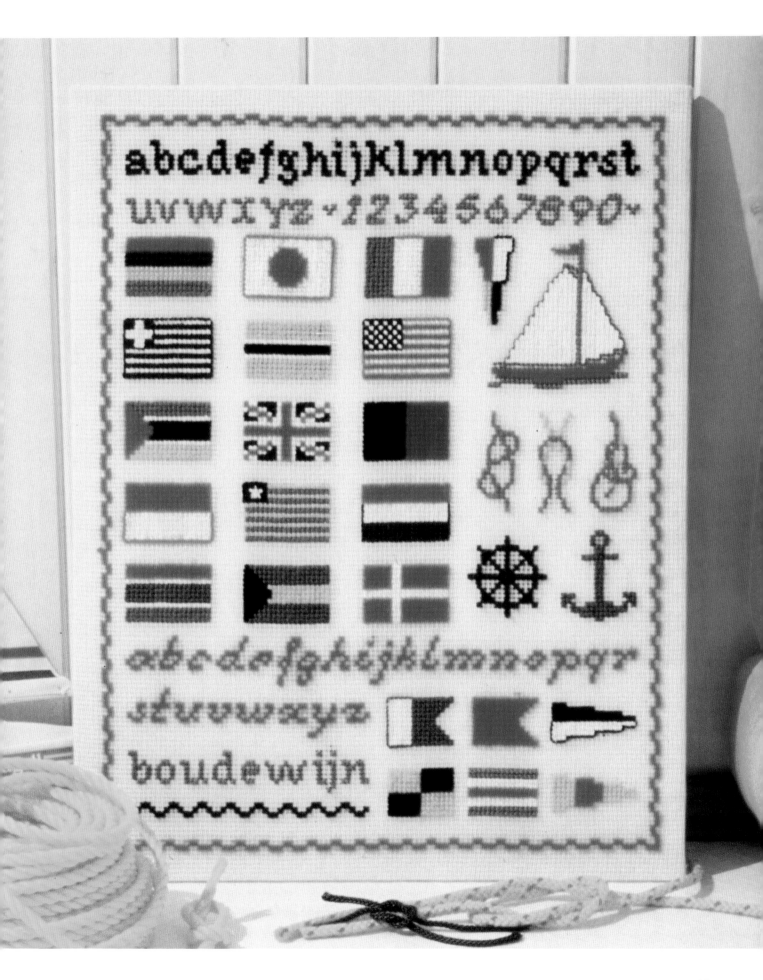

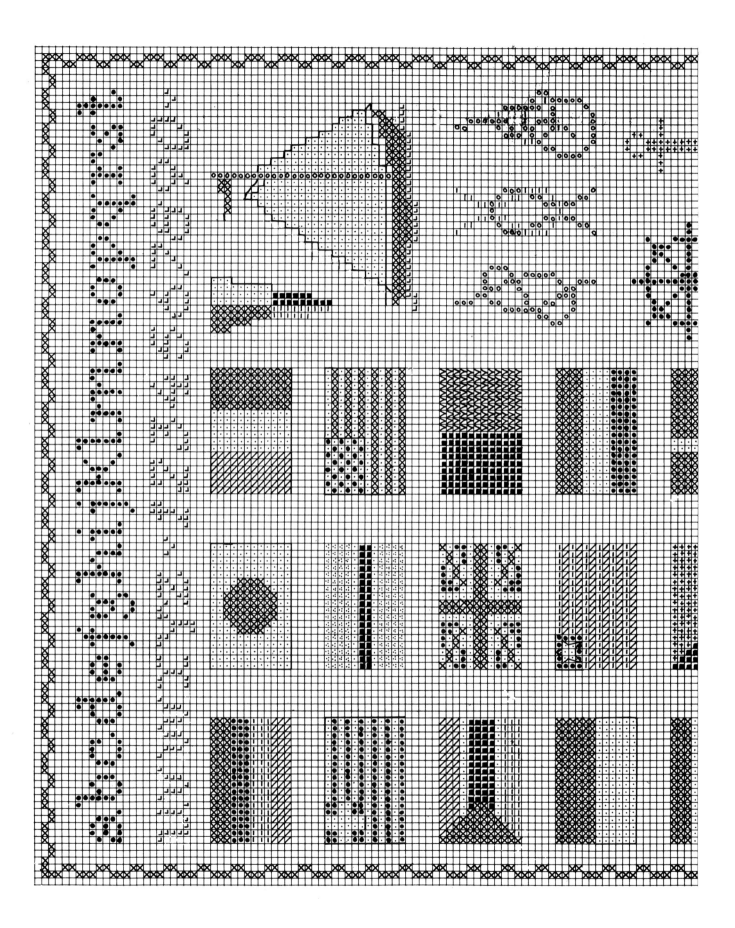

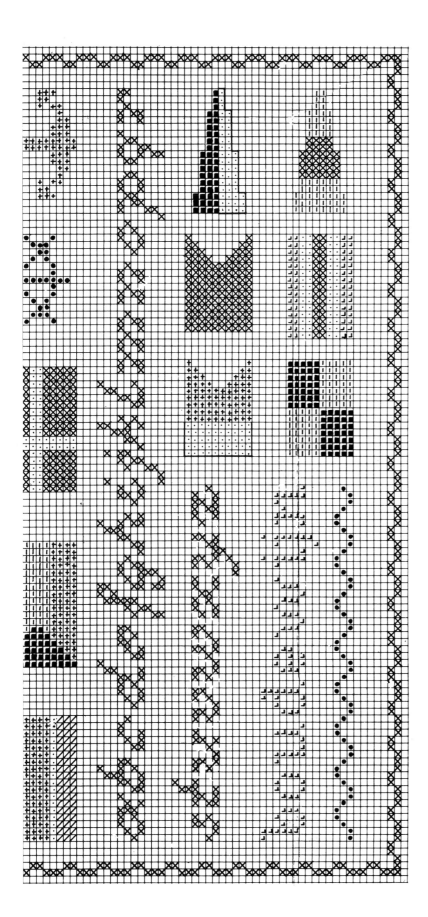

KEY TO CHART

	DMC Floss	Anchor Floss	DMC Cotton
• = white	white	1	white
■ = black	310	403	2310
○ = light toast	436	1045	2767
— = medium yellow	444	290	2444
✕ = light red	666	46	2666
▷ = carmine	815	44	2815

	DMC Floss	Anchor Floss	DMC Cotton
● = dark navy	820	134	2820
∴ = light delft	828	975	2828
╱ = dark mint green	911	205	2911
+ = dark peacock blue	995	410	2995
L = peacock blue	996	433	2996

Flower Basket Samplers

"In the country life of America there are many moments when a woman can have recourse to nothing but her needle for employment."

—THOMAS JEFFERSON TO HIS DAUGHTER MARTHA, 1787

EMBROIDERY MEASUREMENTS

Large sampler: 17 x 20-3/4 in. (43.5 x 53 cm)

Small sampler: 14-1/2 x 16-1/4 in. (37 x 41.5 cm)

MATERIALS

For the large sampler, 25-1/4 x 33 in. (65 x 85 cm) and for the small sampler 21-1/2 x 23-1/2 in. (55 x 60 cm) of white linen with 30 threads per inch (12 per cm); embroidery floss as indicated on the key to the charts; matching frames, if desired.

DIRECTIONS

After marking the horizontal and vertical center of the fabric with basting thread, cross-stitch the motifs according to each chart, using two strands of floss over two threads of linen for each stitch.

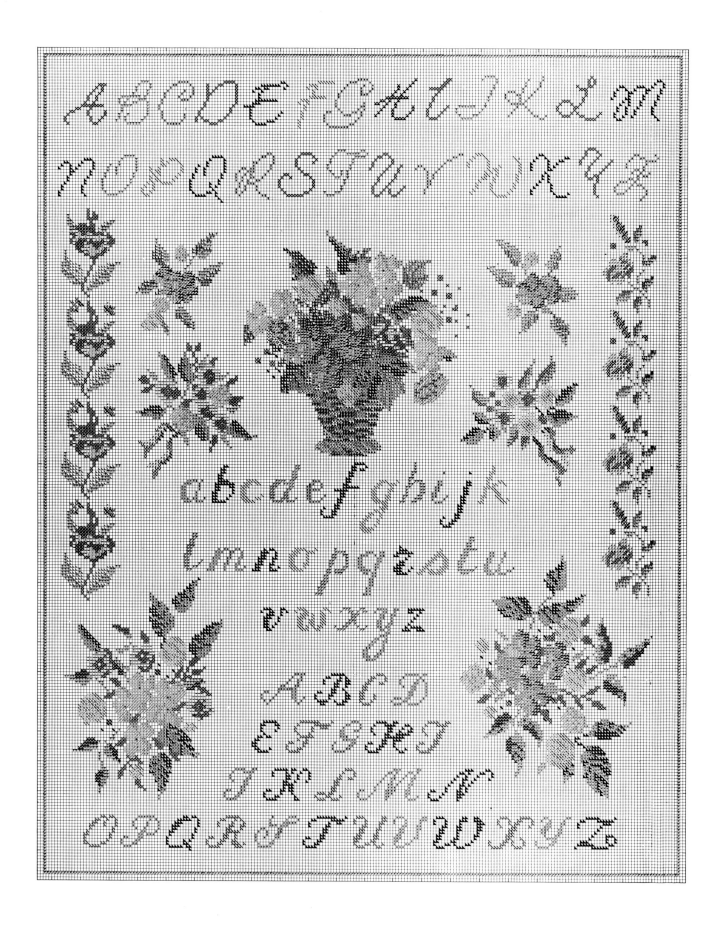

		DMC	Anchor
●	= medium wine	223	895
◺	= medium light wine	224	894
◸	= light wine	225	892
◹	= plum	316	969
✕	= medium jade	368	214
◿	= tan	437	362
◺	= light moss green	472	842
◹	= light pine	503	875
◿	= light jade	504	213
●	= gray green	522	860
Z	= medium desert	612	832
I	= light harvest	613	956
◹	= very light desert	644	831

		DMC	Anchor
∴	= camel	676	891
•	= very light ecru	712	926
∴	= medium peach	744	301
∷	= light tan	738	361
◿	= med. lt. terra cotta	758	337
−	= very lt. loden green	772	259
_	= pink	776	24
O	= wine	778	893
L	= copper	945	881
◻	= medium light beige	950	4146
◿	= light copper	951	880
▶	= medium moss green	3012	844
●	= moss green	3013	843

		DMC	Anchor
◣	= med. light amethyst	3041	871
H	= amethyst	3042	870
∨	= light watermelon	3326	36
N	= very light avocado	3348	264
T	= lt. avocado (Anchor)	3348	265
◻	= light loden green	3364	260
◿	= light lilac	3609	95
∴	= very light coral	3713	968
=	= light amethyst	3743	869
◦•	= light beige	3774	778
+	= medium beige	3779	868

Memorial Sampler

FROM AN EARLY NINETEENTH-CENTURY SAMPLER:

"O may I seize the transient hour
Improve each moment as it flies
Lifes a short summer—man a flower
He dies—Alas—how soon he dies
Wrought by Clarinda Parker aged 13 years
August 3 Anno Domini 1824"

EMBROIDERY MEASUREMENTS

20-1/2 x 24-1/4 in. (52.5 x 62.5 cm)

MATERIALS

29-1/4 x 33 in. (75 x 85 cm) of ecru linen with 30 threads per inch (12 per cm); embroidery floss as indicated on the key to the chart; frame (optional).

DIRECTIONS

After marking the horizontal and vertical center of the fabric with basting thread, cross-stitch the sampler according to the chart using two strands of floss over two threads of fabric for each stitch.

Embroider the appropriate initials and dates in the motifs using the upper alphabet. Fill in the little areas in the peacock's tail with vertical satin stitches—the colors are indicated in each little area. For the peacock's feet, first work all the half-crosses in yellow one way, and then, working in the other direction, stitch the half-crosses over them in black to create complete cross-stitches.

Design Note: Samplers stitched in someone's memory were common in the eighteenth and nineteenth centuries. If you wish, use small beads to embroider your own initials in the center of the flower wreath, and a date of your own choosing in the lowest motif, using the upper alphabet.

KEY TO CHART

	DMC	Anchor		DMC	Anchor		DMC	Anchor		DMC	Anchor
■ = black	310	403	= camel	676	891	∴ = very light beige	948	1011
◩ = medium dark beige	407	914	◭ = olive green	734	279	◻ = light khaki	3013	842
◣ = dark fog	451	233	⊥ = light sand	739	885	► = dark tawny	3021	905
∴ = chartreuse	471	255	⌐ = medium saffron	834	874	◱ = linen	3033	391
● = medium dark pine	501	878	◰ = dark fawn	840	379	◹ = medium light sand	3046	887
✕ = medium pine	502	877	▣ = medium fawn	841	378	◢ = med. lt. sand/black	3046/310	887/403
◥ = medium dark sand	610	889	○ = medium ecru	842	388	S = medium copper	3064	883
⊠ = very dark fawn	632	936	◩ = dark terra cotta	918	341	◣ = avocado	3346	267
= = dark linen	640	393	● = dark aquamarine	924	851	● = med. dk. loden green	3363	262
⌣ = medium linen	642	392	∴ = med. lt. aquamarine	926	850			
· = very light desert	644	830	∴ = light aquamarine	927	849			

38

Circus Sampler

"Dear mother I am young and cannot show
such work as I unto your goodness owe
Be pleased to smile on this my small endeavour
Ill strive to learn and be obedient ever....
Mary Ann Body
her work in y 9
year of her age 1789"

FINISHED MEASUREMENTS

21-3/4 x 27-1/2 in. (56 x 71 cm)

EMBROIDERY MEASUREMENTS

19-1/2 x 25-1/4 in. (50 x 65 cm)

MATERIALS

27 x 33 in. (69.5 x 85 cm) of Aida cloth with 11 thread groups
per inch (4 to 4.5 per cm); embroidery floss as indicated on the
key to the chart; frame (optional).

DIRECTIONS

Mark the horizontal and vertical center of the fabric with basting
thread. Cross-stitch the motif according to the chart, using three
strands of floss over one thread group of fabric for each stitch.

Embroider in outline stitch over completed cross-stitch, using
two strands of floss:

- around the horses in gray #318 or #399;
- around the girl in the ring in medium melon #3340 or #329;
  around the lions in desert #611 or #898;
- and around all remaining figures with black #310 or #403.

Use black #310 or #403 to satin stitch the lions' noses and to
embroider all eyes in French knots.

WITH CHILDREN IN MIND

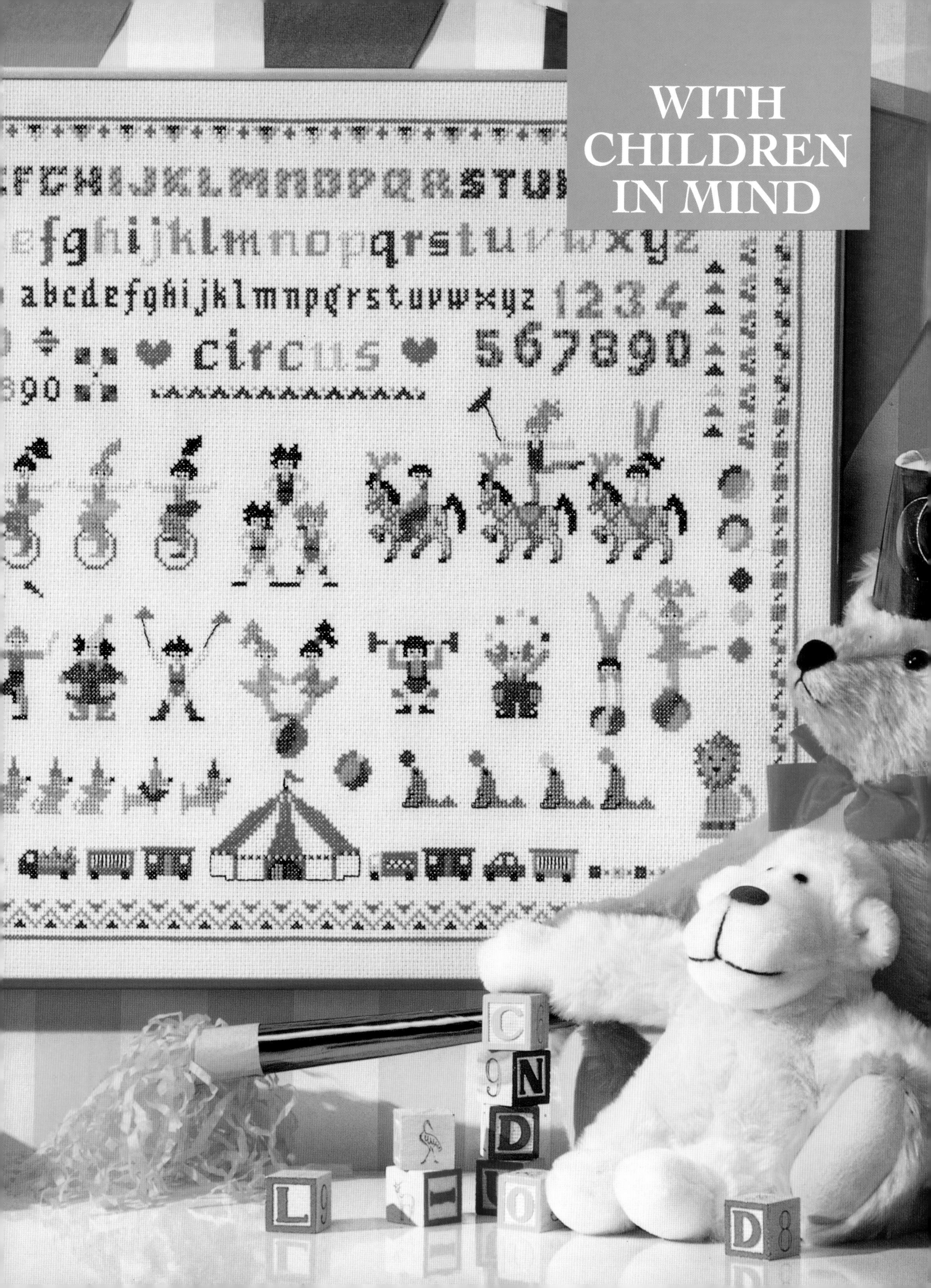

KEY TO CHART

		DMC	Anchor
·	= white	white	1
■	= black	310	403
▨	= gray	318	399
⦂	= medium nutmeg	422	373
●	= desert	611	898
▽	= light red	666	46
Z	= dark bottle green	701	227
∩	= light camel	729	890
‖	= silver	762	234
+	= medium dark topaz	783	308
⊠	= light navy	797	132
O	= medium cobalt	809	130
◺	= medium rose	893	41
╱	= dark pink	894	26
⋮⋮	= light copper	951	880
◿	= medium jonquil	973	297
⋁	= peacock blue	996	433
⦂	= medium melon	3340	329

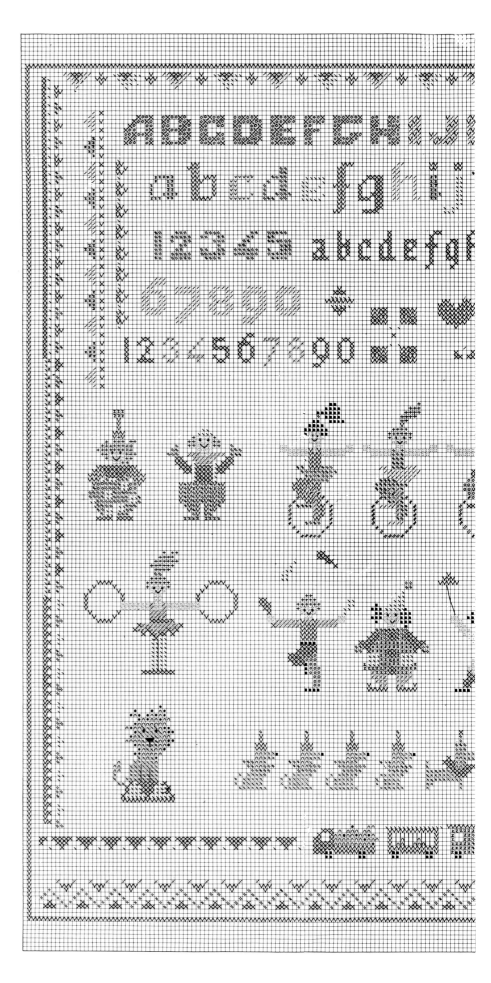

Blue Birth Sampler

"Almighty power whose tender care did infancy protect,
Let riper years thy favour share and every step direct
Rachel Ellicott
1827"

FINISHED MEASUREMENTS

14-3/4 x 19 in. (38 x 48.5 cm)

EMBROIDERY MEASUREMENTS

11-3/4 x 15-3/4 in. (30 x 40.5 cm)

MATERIALS

19 x 19 in. (49 x 49 cm) of white linen with 25 threads per inch (10 per cm); two skeins of light blue embroidery floss (DMC #3753 or Anchor #1031); white embroidery cotton #20 and #25; a matching frame, if desired.

DIRECTIONS

Use basting thread to mark the horizontal and vertical center of the fabric. Embroider the motif according to the chart, using two strands of floss for each stitch. Work each cross-stitch over two threads of linen and each star stitch over four threads.

In the open area, embroider the name and birth date. Embroider the name twenty threads above the date. (The European-style date here lists the month first.)

For the openwork border, use embroidery cotton #25 to work a ladder hemstitch (see the Appendix), gathering four threads for each stitch. Work a small openwork row between the name and cursive letters and large openwork above and below the embroidery work, as shown in the photo, over eight threads.

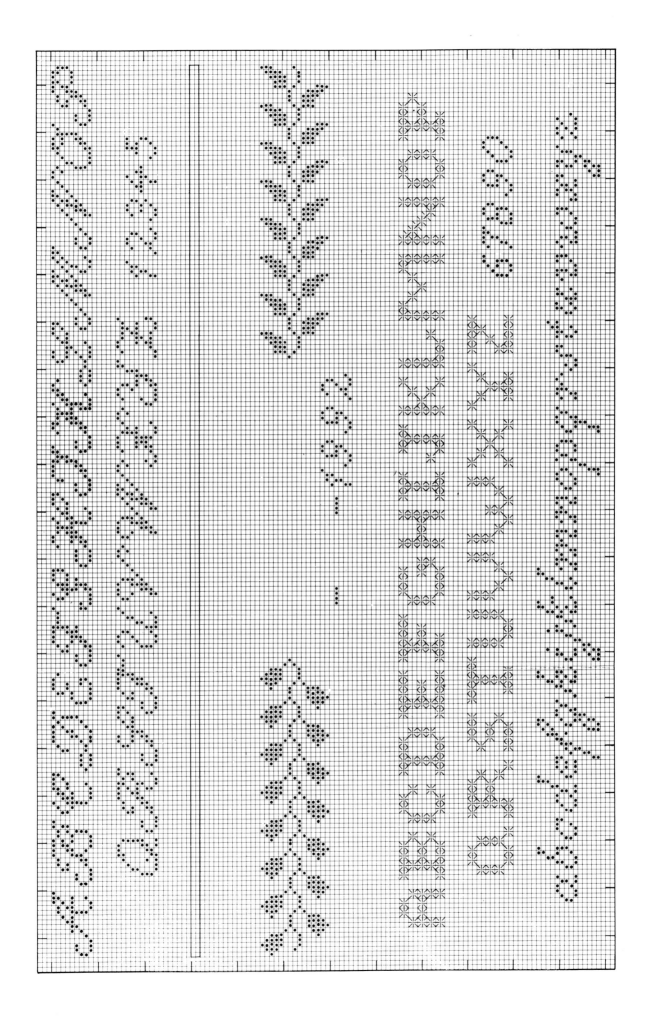

Paper Doll Samplers

FROM TWELVE-YEAR-OLD MARY RICHARDSON'S 1783 SAMPLER:

*"This Needle Work Of Mine Can Tell When A
Child Is Learned Well By My Parents I Was
Tought Not To Spend My Time For Nought"*

FINISHED MEASUREMENTS

16-1/4 x 16-1/4 in. (41.5 x 41.5 cm) each

EMBROIDERY MEASUREMENTS

11-1/4 x 11-1/4 in. (29 x 29 cm) each

MATERIALS

For each sampler, 19-1/2 x 19-1/2 in. (50 x 50 cm) of linen with 25 threads per inch (10 per cm); embroidery floss as indicated on the key to the chart plus dark brown #838 or #380 for the boy only; a wooden frame (optional).

DIRECTIONS

For one sampler, after marking the horizontal and vertical center of the fabric with basting thread, cross-stitch the motif according to the chart, using two strands of floss over two threads of linen for each stitch.

When stitching the border, embroider the name in the center top border and a birth date or other iden-

tifier in the center bottom border, if you wish. (See the section "Starting Out" for centering tips.) Either design your own letters and numbers or adapt those from an alphabet in another sampler in the book. (The European-style date here lists the month first.)

Embroider in outline stitch over completed cross-stitch using two strands of floss over two threads of linen.

For the girl:
- the mouth and the hat in medium dark salmon #350 or #11;
- the body and face in light salmon #353 or #6;
- and the white tabs of the clothes in ocean blue #793 or #176.

For the boy:
- the mouth in dark salmon #817 or #13;
- the body and face in light salmon #353 or #6;
- the hats and the white tabs of the clothes in navy #796 or #133;
- and the bear in dark brown #838 or #380.

KEY TO CHART

		DMC	Anchor
•	= white	white	1
◆	= medium dark salmon	350	11
○	= light salmon	353	6
+	= dark mocha	433	357
□	= medium light teal	598	167

GIRL

		DMC	Anchor
△	= light topaz	725	305
●	= ocean blue	793	176
/	= very light beige	948	1011
−	= light watermelon	3326	36

KEY TO CHART

BOY

		DMC	Anchor			DMC	Anchor
•	= white	white	1	△	= light topaz	725	305
○	= light salmon	353	6	●	= navy	796	133
+	= dark mocha	433	357	◆	= dark salmon	817	13
□	= medium light teal	598	167	/	= very light beige	948	1011
–	= dark bottle green	701	227				

Bows Birth Sampler

"Honor thy mother
For her arms
Secur'd thee from
A thousand harms.
Charlotte Frobisher,
aged 9
1805."

EMBROIDERY MEASUREMENTS

20 x 22-1/4 in. (51 x 57 cm)

MATERIALS

29-1/4 x 31-1/4 in. (75 x 80 cm) of Hardanger cloth with 11 threads per inch (4.5 per cm); embroidery floss as indicated on the key to the chart; frame (optional).

DIRECTIONS

After marking the horizontal and vertical center of the fabric with basting thread, cross-stitch the motif according to the chart using three strands of floss over one thread of fabric for each stitch. Use the alphabet and numbers in the sampler to substitute the appropriate name and date. (The European-style date on the pictured sampler lists the month first.)

KEY TO CHART

		DMC	Anchor
·	= white	white	1
■	= black	310	403
✕	= jade	320	215
●	= medium watermelon	335	38
◆	= light topaz	725	305
◇	= light jonquil	727	293
○	= pink	776	24
✕	= light sapphire	813	161
✗	= very dark delft	825	979
▣	= sapphire	826	162
☐	= medium glacier blue	827	159
△	= medium blossom pink	899	52
▲	= forest green	912	209
△	= light lime	966	240
◉	= dark tangerine	971	316
⊙	= light watermelon	3326	36

Nursery Sampler

FROM A SALEM, MASSACHUSETTS, SAMPLER,
BY NABY DANE, AGE TWELVE:

"Naby Dane Her Sampler
  Wrought June The 27 1789
  Born July The 19 1777
  Next Unto God
  Dear Parents I Address MySelf To you
  In Humble Thankfulness
  For All your Care
  And Charge On me"

FINISHED MEASUREMENTS

20-1/2 x 27 in. (52.5 x 69.5 cm)

EMBROIDERY MEASUREMENTS

15-1/4 x 21-1/2 in. (39 x 55 cm)

MATERIALS

25-1/4 x 31-1/4 in. (65 x 80 cm) of Hardanger fabric with 22-1/2 threads
per inch (9 per cm); embroidery floss as indicated on the key to the
chart; if desired, a frame 20-1/2 x 27 in. (52.5 x 69.5 cm).

DIRECTIONS

Mark the horizontal and vertical center of the fabric with basting thread.
Cross-stitch the motif according to the chart, using three strands of floss
over two threads of fabric for each stitch.

Insert the desired name in the space at the bottom center of the chart,
using letters from the upper alphabet, with the birth date centered above
it, using whichever numbers you choose (see the section "Starting Out"
for spacing tips). (The birth date in the picture lists the month first,
European style.)

KEY TO CHART

		DMC	Anchor
■	= black	310	403
●	= brick	356	5975
✕	= med. dark pine	501	878
○	= med. light copper	758	882
◇	= med. saffron	834	874
☐	= denim blue	932	920

Mama and Papa Bear Samplers

FROM A 1769 SAMPLER:

*"When in Love I do commence
May it be with a man of sense
Brisk and arey may he be
Free from a spirit of jealousy."*

EMBROIDERY MEASUREMENTS

11 x 11 in. (28 x 28 cm)

MATERIALS

For each portrait, 15-1/2 x 15-1/2 in. (40 x 40 cm) of counted cross-stitch fabric with 25 threads per inch (10 per cm); embroidery floss as indicated on the key to the charts; frames, if desired.

DIRECTIONS

After marking the vertical and horizontal center of the fabric with basting thread, cross-stitch the motif according to the charts, using four strands of floss over four threads of fabric.

Embroider in outline stitch over completed cross-stitch, following the key for outline stitches and the chart.

KEY TO CHARTS

		DMC	Anchor
⠰	= ecru	ecru	387
⊠	= black	310	403
+	= red	321	9046
▢	= medium watermelon	335	38
●	= dark mocha	433	357
◇	= brown	434	370
⟍	= chartreuse	470	256
—	= sand	677	886
⟋	= light topaz	725	305
○	= dark topaz	781	309
•	= topaz	783	307
▼	= ocean blue	793	176
╱	= light ocean blue	794	175
◆	= dark coffee	898	360
‖	= medium sand	3045	888
△	= light denim	3752	343

Outline Stitches

		DMC	Anchor
∿∿	= black	310	403
⌣⌣	= red	321	9046
– – –	= dark mocha	433	357
———	= med. ocean blue	792	177
— — —	= ocean blue	793	176
⊢⊢⊢⊢	= dark fawn	840	379

Carnival Sampler

FROM AN 1800 SAMPLER BY PATTY POLK,
AGE TEN, KENT, MARYLAND:

*"Patty Polk did this
and she hated every stitch
she did in it.
She loves to read
much more."*

EMBROIDERY MEASUREMENTS

46-1/2 x 26 in. (119 x 67 cm)

MATERIALS

54-1/2 x 35 in. (140 x 90 cm) of cream-colored cotton with 17.5 threads per inch (7 per cm.); embroidery floss as indicated on the key to the chart; black DMC pearl cotton #8 or the equivalent; a frame or a piece of chipboard 46-1/2 x 26 in. (119 x 67 cm), if desired.

DIRECTIONS

Mark the horizontal and vertical center of the fabric with basting thread, then cross-stitch the carnival motifs according to the chart, using four strands of floss over two threads of fabric for each stitch.

Outline stitch over completed cross-stitch, using three strands of floss:

- dark red orange #606 or #335 for the mouths;
- for the whirler on the right, dark red orange #606 or #335 for the middle section and dark jonquil #972 or #298 in the scallops around the roof;
- navy #796 or #133 for the pigtailed girl at the lower right, the boy with the yo-yo, the girl with the balloon, and the boy with the dark red orange cap;
- and the remaining outline stitches in black #310 or #403.

For the lines under the children, use black #310 or #403, navy #796 or #133, or light charcoal #317 or #400.

Make long straight stitches in black pearl cotton #8 for the lines of the whirlers, the balloons, and the yo-yo.

Embroider the border in satin stitch with six strands of floss. (Refer to the border chart in the upper right corner of the large chart.) For one square on the chart, make two small satin stitches over two fabric threads. Then use one strand of the same color to make a row of running stitches below the satin stitches. Beginning at the lower right corner of the border, embroider sixty-seven blue triangles along the bottom border. After working the lower left corner,

embroider thirty-six blue triangles along the left side border. Repeat for the top and right side.

If you wish, frame the finished needlework or stretch it over the chipboard.

Design Note:
Each of the figures can also be made as an individual picture for small samplers, cards, towels, clothing, soft blocks, and other children's items.

KEY TO CHART

		DMC	Anchor			DMC	Anchor			DMC	Anchor
•	= white	white	1	⬗	= light charcoal	317	400	⊠	= dark red orange	606	335
▼	= dark bark	300	352	▽	= gray	318	399	∷	= light desert	613	831
∣	= yellow	307	289	◺	= light gray	415	398	o	= emerald	702	239
■	= black	310	403	∨	= light rosebud pink	604	55	—	= medium light copper	758	882

	DMC	Anchor			DMC	Anchor			DMC	Anchor
∴ = silver	762	234	N = dark sapphire	825	164	▢ = peacock blue	996	433
● = navy	796	133	∴ = copper	945	881	L = medium sand	3045	888
◣ = medium blue	798	142	Z = dark tangerine	970	316			
∴ = light cobalt	809	130	╱ = dark jonquil	972	298			

Butterfly Birth Sampler

FROM A NINETEENTH-CENTURY SAMPLER
STITCHED IN PETERBOROUGH, NEW HAMPSHIRE:

"Youth the spring time of our years
Short the rapid scene appears
let's improve the fleeting hours
Virtue's noblest fruits be ours
Wrought by Sally Abbot aged 11 years.
June 6th 1818"

FINISHED MEASUREMENTS

17-1/2 x 17-1/2 in. (45 x 45 cm)

MATERIALS

White Hardanger cloth 22 x 22 in. (56.5 x 56.5 cm) with 23 double threads per inch (9 per cm); embroidery floss as indicated on the key to the chart; frame, if desired.

DIRECTIONS

After marking the horizontal and vertical center of the fabric with basting thread, cross-stitch the motif according to the chart, using three strands of floss over two double threads of fabric for each stitch.

Outline stitch over completed cross-stitch, using three strands of floss:
- very dark bark #400 or #351 around the cat;
- red orange #606 or #334 around the windows of the house;
- and black #310 or #403 for the remaining figures.

Work satin stitches for the animals' mouths (see the photo) using three strands of black #310 or #403. Stem stitch the whiskers of the rabbits and cat with two strands of black #310 or #403, and the rooster's feet with three strands of light emerald #700 or #228.

Use the alphabet and numbers in the sampler to substitute the appropriate name and date. (The European-style date on the pictured sampler lists the month first.)

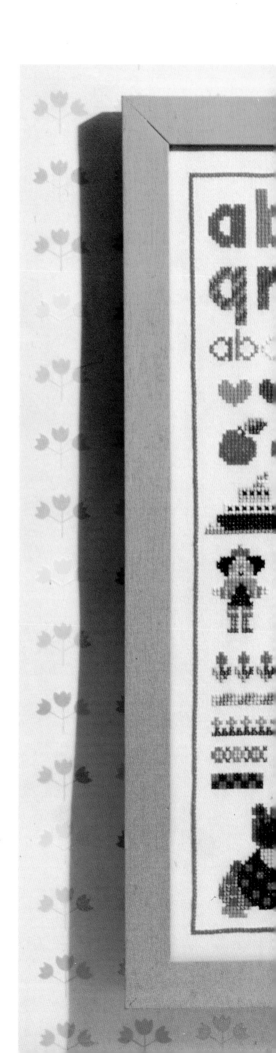

defghijklmnop
tuvwxyz123456789
123456890·0
fghijklmnopqrstuvwxyz

peter

13·10·1981

KEY TO CHART

		DMC	Anchor
·	= white	white	1
◤	= black	310	403
⚲	= gray	318	399
◗	= dark red	321	47
◖	= very dark bark	400	351
⊡	= medium yellow	444	290
◺	= violet	552	99
●	= medium magenta	603	62
◙	= red orange	606	334
▽	= light desert	613	831
N	= light emerald	700	228
∴	= light jonquil	727	293
⊠	= dark orange	741	304
◣	= navy	796	133
◿	= medium glacier blue	827	159
▼	= dark coffee	898	360
S	= parrot green	905	257
O	= dark chartreuse	907	255
∷	= copper	945	881
◹	= dark melon	947	330
⊠	= peacock blue	996	433
◿	= medium sand	3045	888

Schoolroom Sampler

"While I with care my work pursue
And to my book my mind apply
Ill keep my teachrs love in view
And guard my way with watch
ful eye…
Wrought by Rebecca J Wild
Charlestown Jan 1 1831
Aged 10 years"

FINISHED MEASUREMENTS

18-3/4 x 28 in. (48 x 72)

EMBROIDERY MEASUREMENTS

17-1/2 x 27 in. (45 x 69 cm)

MATERIALS

25-1/4 x 35 in. (65 x 90 cm) of white double-thread canvas with 7-1/2 mesh holes per inch (3 per cm); DMC embroidery cotton (or its equivalent) as indicated on the key to the chart plus ecru and pale blue #2828; (optional) frame or pressboard 17-1/2 x 27 in. (45 x 69 cm).

DIRECTIONS

Mark the horizontal and vertical center of the canvas with basting thread. Using one strand of embroidery cotton over one mesh hole for each stitch, cross-stitch the motif according to the chart.

Use other stitches for the following figures (see the Appendix):
- for the baseboard, use vertical satin stitches;
- for the books, use horizontal satin stitches;
- for the windowsills, use horizontal and vertical satin stitches;
- for the curtain rod, use vertical satin stitches over a long straight stitch;
- for the little red flowers in the plant, make French knots;
- for the drapes, use half cross-stitches over a long straight stitch;

- for the blackboard, use half cross-stitches and then run one strand in diagonal lines beneath them;
- for the sky, use running stitches in pale blue #2828 cotton: run one strand through the large mesh holes (up one, down one) and another strand through the narrow mesh holes to create a woven effect (refer to the photo);
- for the floor, use ecru running stitches for fourteen rows below the bottom line of cross-stitches; run two strands through the large mesh holes and

one strand through the narrow mesh holes
- for the teacher's necklace, use one dark blue strand in which you make knots to simulate beads.

Outline stitch over completed cross-stitch with one strand of cotton:
- turquoise #2996 around the blue-green bag;
- dark blue #2825 around the turquoise bag;
- blue #2827 in and around the dark blue bags;
- dark blue #2825 for the numbers on the clock;
- beige #2613 for the line along the windowsills and

the bear's ear;
- dark brown #2839 for the teacher's eyebrows, around the desks and bookshelves, and around the animals (except the goat and the duck's head);
- and brown #2609 for all other outline stitches.

If you wish, frame the embroidery or stretch it around the pressboard.

KEY TO CHART

		DMC Cotton			DMC Cotton			DMC Cotton
·	= white	white	◢	= green	2561	∷	= pink	2758
●	= black	2310	◹	= blue green	2595	▼	= dark blue	2825
⸰∕	= gray	2318	⊠	= brown	2609	∟	= blue	2827
+	= red	2349	‖	= beige	2613	∨	= dark brown	2839
○	= light green	2471	◡	= yellow	2727	╱	= turquoise	2996

68

Pastel Birth Sampler

FROM A 1681 SAMPLER BY MARGARET LUCUS:

"My father hitherto hath done his best to make me a workewoman above the rest. Margreet Lucuh 1681 bezng ten year old come July the first."

FINISHED MEASUREMENTS

15-1/2 x 18-3/4 in. (40 x 48 cm)

EMBROIDERY MEASUREMENTS

10-1/2 x 13-3/4 in. (27 x 35.5 cm)

Note: The motifs can be extended to accommodate a longer name.

MATERIALS

Hardanger cloth 19-1/2 x 23-1/2 in. (50 x 60 cm) with 23 thread groups per inch (9 per cm); embroidery floss as indicated on the key to the chart; frame (optional).

DIRECTIONS

Cross-stitch the motif according to the chart using three strands of floss over two fabric threads for each stitch. Begin embroidering in the upper right-hand corner 2-1/2 in. (6.5 cm) from the edge of the fabric. Repeat motif 1 four times. Embroider the rest of the sampler one set of motifs at a time, so that stitching for each set ends at the same place on the left side of the sampler (see photo).

To embroider the name and date, mark the center by stitching a line of basting down the middle of your piece, using the top motif as a guide. Center the name and date where "1993" appears on the chart, according to the instructions in the section "Starting Out." (You can choose letters from an alphabet on one of the other samplers in the book or design your own.) Embroider the name and date first, then embroider the motif on each side. (The pictured sampler lists the month first, European style.)

When you have completed all eight sets of motifs, embroider the border according to the chart.

KEY TO CHART

		DMC	Anchor
☐	= medium jade	368	214
•	= camel	676	891
☒	= light coral	761	1021
●	= ocean blue	793	176
○	= light ocean blue	794	175
✗	= dark blush	3733	75

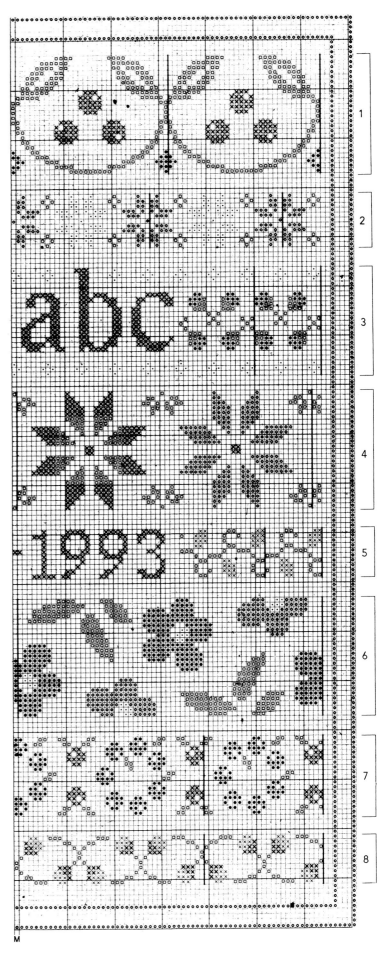

Home Sweet Home Sampler

"Tell me ye knowing and discerning few
Where I may find a Friend both firm and true
Who dares stand by me when in deep distress
And then his Love and Friendship dost express
Mary Ann Richards her Work
June The First 1800"

FINISHED MEASUREMENTS

13 x 16-1/2 in. (33.5 x 42 cm)

EMBROIDERY MEASUREMENTS

11-3/4 x 14-3/4 in. (30 x 38 cm)

MATERIALS

21-1/2 x 23-1/2 in. (55 x 60 cm) of linen with 25 threads per inch (10 per cm); DMC or Anchor embroidery floss as indicated in the key to the chart plus juniper #367 or #217, raspberry #3687 or #68, and delft #334 or #977; frame, if desired.

DIRECTIONS

After marking the horizontal and vertical center of the fabric with basting thread, cross-stitch the sampler using two strands of floss over two threads of linen for each stitch.

Embroider in outline stitch over completed cross-stitch using one strand of floss:

- around the plum flowers with raspberry #3687 or #68;
- in and around the light delft flowers and the light seafoam centers of the blooming roses in delft #334 or #977;
- along the roof, the lower edge of the house, the window frames, the bench, the flower pots, the light topaz flowers, and in and around the basket with pine #503 or #876.

Embroider all remaining outline stitches in juniper #367 or #217.

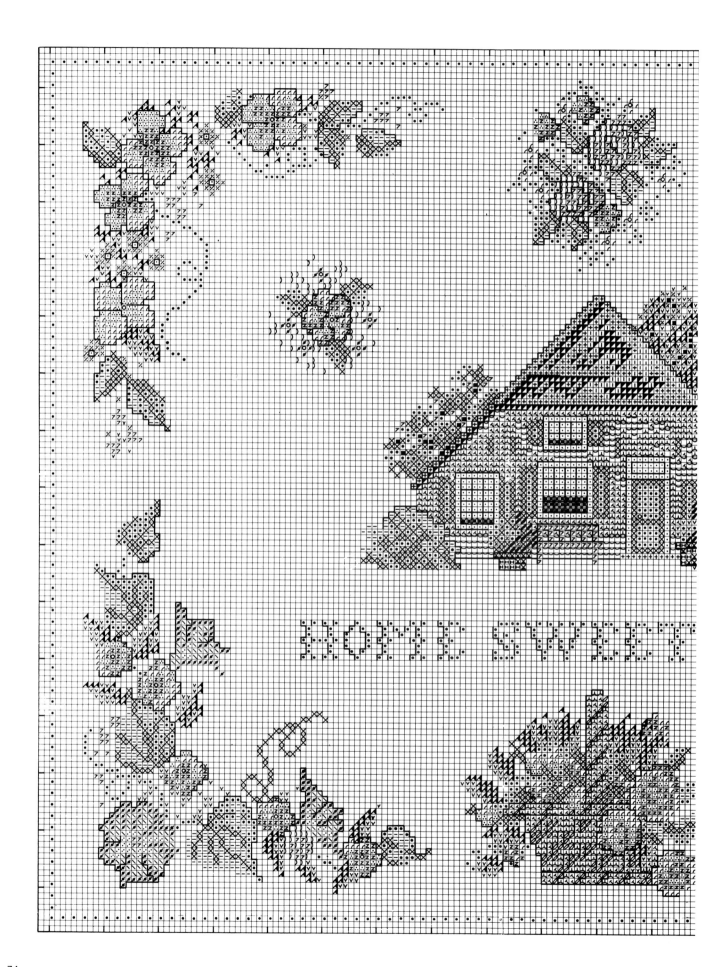

KEY TO CHART

		DMC	Anchor
•	= white	white	1
�	= off-white	white	2
✗	= medium wine	223	895
◢	= light wine	225	892
Z	= plum	316	969
⊠	= jade	320	216
●	= medium jade	368	214
H	= light cinnamon	402	347
◪	= medium nutmeg	422	373
7	= tan	437	362
◤	= medium pine	502	877
◀	= pine	503	876
∨	= light pine	504	875
◣	= pewter	646	8581
◁	= sand	677	886
O	= light topaz	725	305
◔	= light sand	739	885
◗	= peach	745	300
—	= light loden green	772	259
∴	= light plum	778	968
▯	= light linen	822	390
◿	= light delft	828	975
◤	= terra cotta	921	338
•	= denim blue	932	920
∴	= light seafoam	3072	847
+	= light tawny	3782	899
■	= dark linen	3790	393
◼	= charcoal	3799	236

Caribbean Sampler

"Mary Bosworth, lately from London, takes this method to inform the public, that she has opened a school...wherein she teaches young masters and misses to read...learns young ladies plain work, samplairs, Dresden flowering on cat gut."

—THE *NEW YORK MERCURY*, 20 MAY 1765

EMBROIDERY MEASUREMENTS

37 x 37 in. (95 x 95 cm)

MATERIALS

44 x 44 in. (113 x 113 cm) of ecru linen with 13 threads per inch (5 per cm); Anchor embroidery wool (or its equivalent) as indicated on the key to the chart; frame, if desired.

DIRECTIONS

Mark the horizontal and vertical center of the fabric with basting thread, then embroider the motifs within the borders in cross-stitch, using one strand of wool over two threads of fabric for each stitch.

Next, embroider the lines between the squares in Rumanian stitch, using one strand of wool (see the Appendix). Stitches should be one thread high and ten threads wide.

Embroider the two red outlines in flannel stitch (see the Appendix) using one strand of wool, with stitches eight threads high and four threads wide. Work the corners as shown in the photo.

KEY TO CHART

		Anchor Yarn
＼	= rose	63
▼	= purple	107
◼	= blue	133
∴	= light blue	159
◢	= dark green	229
⊠	= green	239
∨	= olive green	279
−	= yellow	295
o	= orange	332
•	= white	402
◼	= black	403
⌐	= turquoise	567
		= pink	642
▽	= brown	650
=	= light brown	742
●	= red	748

Pastry Sampler

FROM AN 1820 SAMPLER BY
ELEANOR MALONE OF MASSACHUSETTS:

"O may I with myself agree
And never covet what i see
content me with an humble shade
My passions tam'd my wishes laid
Wrought by
Eleanor Caroline Malone aged 8 years"

FINISHED MEASUREMENTS

20-1/4 x 23-1/2 in. (52 x 60 cm)

EMBROIDERY MEASUREMENTS

17 x 19-1/2 in. (43.5 x 50 cm)

MATERIALS

28 x 31-1/4 in. (72 x 80 cm) of ecru linen with 25 threads per inch (10 per cm); DMC or Anchor embroidery floss as indicated on the key to the chart plus dark charcoal #535 or #400, dark turquoise #991 or #189, medium grape #3746 or #1030, and charcoal #3799 or #236; for the Hardanger border, Anchor white embroidery cotton #16 and #20 (or the equivalent); a frame, if desired.

DIRECTIONS

Mark the horizontal and vertical center of the fabric with basting thread. Using two strands of floss over two fabric threads for each stitch, cross-stitch the motif according to the chart.

Embroider in outline stitch over completed cross-stitch with one strand of floss:

- the names of the pastries with charcoal #3799 or #236;
- in and around the medium light pewter cake stands and the two chocolate cakes with dark charcoal #535 or #400;
- in and around the rest of the cakes with very dark fawn #632 or #936;
- in and around the upper right cake stand, the little dollops on the cakes, and the cake with the light maroon bow with very dark fawn #632 or #936 and with light toast #436 or #1045, as you prefer;
- in and around the remaining gold-colored stands with light toast #436 or #1045;
- in and around the light green decorations with dark turquoise #991 or #189;
- around the grape bow with medium grape #3746 or #1030;
- around the blossom pink bows, flowers, and decorations with medium watermelon #335 or #38;
- and around the light maroon bow with blossom pink #326 or #59.

81

KEY TO CHART

	DMC	Anchor			DMC	Anchor			DMC	Anchor
· = white	white	1		□ = light pewter	648	900		● = light maroon	961	76
● = blossom pink	326	59		╱ = sand	677	886		O = light rust	977	1002
◢ = medium watermelon	335	38		·· = very light ecru	712	926		◢ = light green	988	243
◣ = grape	340	118		·. = light apricot	722	323		╱ = linen	3033	391
+ = light grape	341	117		□ = light sand	739	885		│ = light seafoam	3072	847
Z = medium jade	368	214		⌐ = peach	745	300		> = very light avocado	3348	264
┬ = light cinnamon	402	347		·· = light peach	746	275		■ = very dark magenta	3350	65
┤ = medium dark beige	407	914		╱ = very lt. loden green	772	259		╱ = blush	3354	74
= = medium nutmeg	422	373		⊠ = medium blossom pink	899	52		·: = very light coral	3713	1020
⊼ = light toast	436	1045		╲ = dark rust	922	1003		╲ = medium pink	3716	25
= = tan	437	362		∩ = medium light beige	950	4146		·: = light blueberry	3747	120
● = very dark fawn	632	936		│ = light copper	951	880		⊠ = dark cocoa	3772	1007
⊿ = medium light pewter	647	1040		╲ = blossom pink	957	50		⊿ = medium cocoa	3773	1008

CHART 1

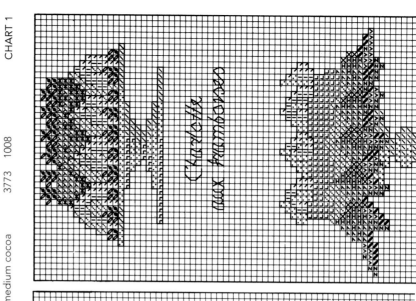

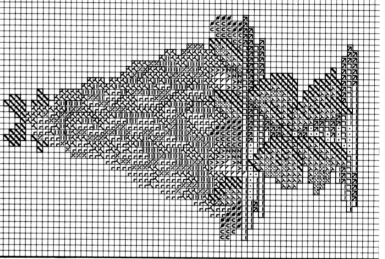

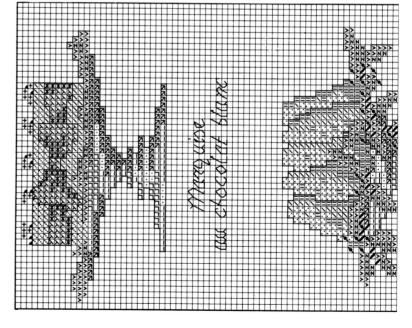

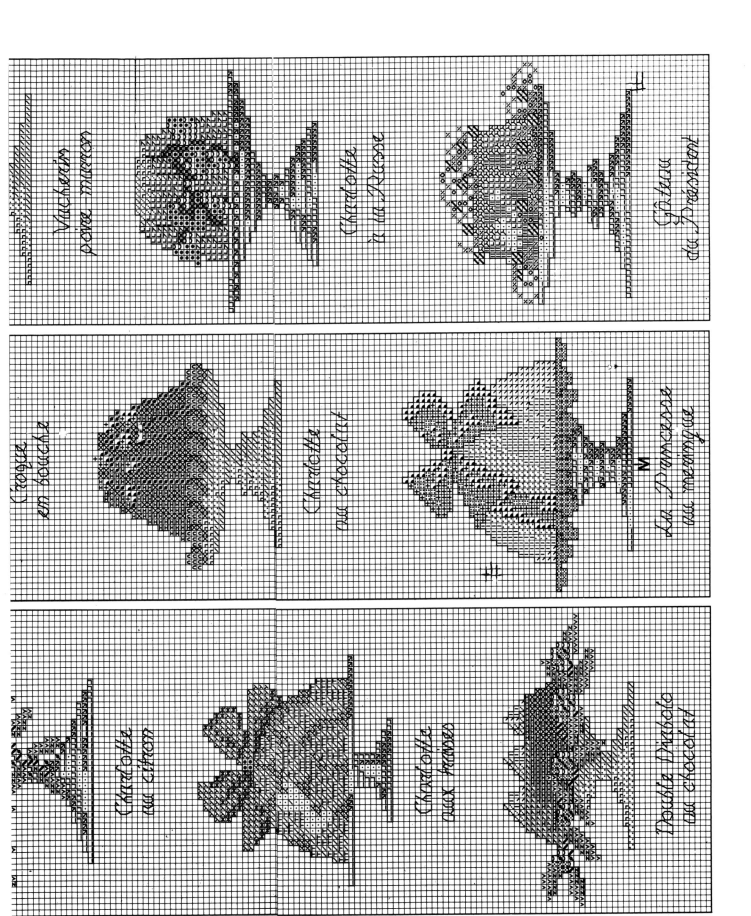

Vacherin poire-marron

Charlotte à la Russe

Gâteau du Fumeur

Croque en bouche

Charlotte au chocolat

La Jonesse au marengo

Charlotte au citron

Charlotte aux pommes

Double Diabolo au chocolat

CHART 2

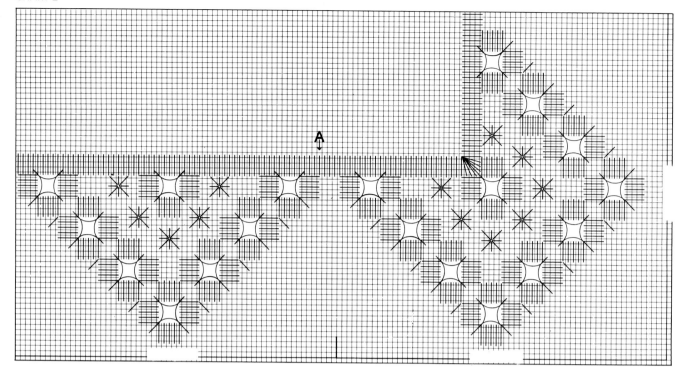

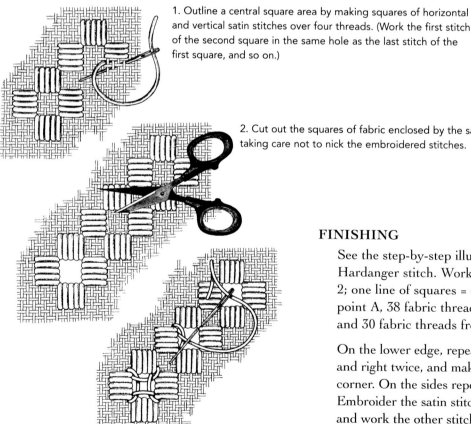

1. Outline a central square area by making squares of horizontal and vertical satin stitches over four threads. (Work the first stitch of the second square in the same hole as the last stitch of the first square, and so on.)

2. Cut out the squares of fabric enclosed by the satin stitching, taking care not to nick the embroidered stitches.

3. Refer to chart 2: decorate the open squares with a filling stitch that runs from corner to corner or with a star stitch.

FINISHING

See the step-by-step illustrations for working the Hardanger stitch. Work the border according to chart 2; one line of squares = one fabric thread. Begin at point A, 38 fabric threads below the center cake stand and 30 fabric threads from point M on chart 1.

On the lower edge, repeat the border motif to the left and right twice, and make a corner motif at each corner. On the sides repeat the border motif six times. Embroider the satin stitches in embroidery cotton #16, and work the other stitches in embroidery cotton #20. Follow the three-step directions for the border, working the satin stitches first, then cutting along the stitching to cut away the inside squares (white squares on chart 2). In the open squares, make filling stitches or star stitches, according to chart 2.

Home Celebration Sampler

FROM AN 1808 MARRIAGE SAMPLER BY MARY LEE:

"But happy they the happiest of their kind!
Whom gentler stars unite, and in one fate
Their hearts, their fortunes,
and their beings blend."

FINISHED MEASUREMENTS

26 x 27-1/4 in. (67 x 70 cm)

**EMBROIDERY
MEASUREMENTS**

21 x 22-1/4 in. (54 x 57 cm)

MATERIALS

36 x 36 in. (92.5 x 92.5 cm) of white
linen with 25 threads per inch
(10 per cm); embroidery floss as
indicated on the key to the chart;
frame, if desired.

DIRECTIONS

Mark the horizontal and vertical
center of the fabric with basting
thread, then cross-stitch the
motif according to the chart.
Use two strands of floss over
two fabric threads for each
cross-stitch.

In the open areas, you may
choose to embroider your own
initials or those of the persons
you wish to celebrate. Choose
from the letters of the alphabet
at the top of the sampler (change
the size to suit your needs; see
the section "Starting Out"). If
you wish, embroider a date
below the upper window of the
house, as shown in the photo.

Embroider in outline stitch over
completed cross-stitch, using
two strands of floss:

- dark mint green #911 or #205
  around the Christmas trees;
- orange #742 or #303 in and
  around the light orange
  flowers;
- medium blossom pink #899 or
  #52 in and around the pink
  and the pink-and-white
  flowers;
- medium spring green #703
  or #238 around the white
  flowers in the border;

Design Note: This sampler makes a special gift for a new home or to celebrate a marriage or partnership or a new family member. The corner motifs reflect the seasons of the year.

- light apricot #722 or #323 around the light orange butterfly and around the light orange flowers beneath it;
- light rust #977 or #363 for the lines that emphasize the ears of wheat;
- gray #318 or #399 around the white flowers near the wheat;
- gray #318 or #399 or medium light amethyst #3041 or #871 for the butterflies' antennas;
- and black #310 or #403 in and around the berries and apples, around the sapphire butterflies, and in the centers of the light orange or light orange-and-white flowers.

KEY TO CHART

	DMC	Anchor			DMC	Anchor
⊡ = white	white	1	⟋ = camel	676	891
⊙ = wine	224	893	▷ = medium spring green	703	238
◣ = black	310	403	◁ = light parrot green	704	256
⟋ = gray	318	399	⟍ = light apricot	722	323
⊢ = light grape	341	117	⊢ = light topaz	725	305
⟍ = medium dark salmon	350	11	⟍ = light jonquil	727	293
C = salmon	352	9	⊡ = light camel	729	890
⟋ = very light lime	369	1043	⟍ = orange	742	303
◤ = very dark topaz	434	310	⟍ = light orange	743	302
⟍ = tan	437	362	⊢ = peach	745	300
⟍ = light chartreuse	472	253	⊡ = light peach	746	386
⊠ = light pewter	648	900	⟍ = light cobalt	775	128

	DMC	Anchor			DMC	Anchor
⌒ = pink	776	24	⟊ = medium jonquil	973	297
N = medium dark topaz	782	308	◤ = medium mocha	975	355
⊡ = light pink	818	23	⟍ = light rust	977	363
✳ = sapphire	826	162	⊠ = light green	988	243
⋰ = medium glacier blue	827	159	⊙ = medium light amethyst	3041	871
⟋ = medium blossom pink	899	52	⟋ = avocado	3346	267
● = dark mint green	911	205	⟍ = medium light avocado	3347	266
⟍ = medium mint green	913	204	⟁ = very light avocado	3348	264
⋰ = dark rust	922	1003	◣ = dark cherry	3705	35
⟍ = denim blue	932	920			
⟋ = copper	945	881			
⊟ = medium light beige	950	4146			

87

Louis XVI Chairs Sampler

FROM MARY MILLER'S 1735 SAMPLER:

"No surplice white the priest could wear
Bandless the bishop must appear
The King without a shirt would be
Did not the needle help all three."

EMBROIDERY MEASUREMENTS

10-1/2 x 13-1/2 in. (27 x 34.5 cm)

MATERIALS

25-1/4 x 29-1/4 in. (65 x 75 cm) of Hardanger cloth with 23 double threads per inch (9 per cm); DMC or Anchor embroidery floss as indicated on the key to the chart plus dark brown #433 or #371, dark moss green #3011 or #846, medium sand #3045 or #888, wheat #869 or #944, and pewter #646 or #8581; a matching frame and mat, if desired.

DIRECTIONS

After marking the horizontal and vertical center of the fabric with basting thread, cross-stitch the motif following the chart, using two strands of floss over two double threads of fabric for each stitch. Where two colors of floss are listed, use one strand of each.

Embroider in outline stitch over completed cross-stitch using one strand of floss. For the bottom row of chairs, outline stitch in and around the wooden frame of the chair on the lower right in pewter #646 or #8581. For the chair at the lower left, use teal #807 or #168 to make the little star in the chair back with four large outline stitches and to top stitch the vertical lines in the seat. Top stitch the horizontal lines in the seat with two strands of brick #356 or #5975. Outline stitch in and around the sofa with medium camel #680 or #901.

Note: To top stitch, hand or machine sew a line of small, closely spaced running stitches on the right side of the fabric.

On the top row, outline stitch in and around the wooden frame of the upper right chair with medium sand #3045 or #888, and in and around the upholstery with aquamarine #3768 or #779. For the chair second from the right, outline stitch the feet with medium bark #301 or #349, in and around the wooden frame with fudge #838 or #380, and in and around the seat with moss green #3012 or #843. For the chair second from the left, outline stitch in and around the wooden frame with dark tawny #3021 or #905, and in and around the seat with two strands of very light turf #3047 or #852. For the armchair in the upper left, outline stitch in and around the wooden frame with dark brown #433 or #371, and in and around the upholstery with brick #356 or #5975.

For the border of the picture, use two strands of medium sand #3045 or #888 to make long outline stitches that angle from left to right, as the chart indicates, two cross-stitches in width and three cross-stitches in height.

KEY TO CHART

		DMC	Anchor
◣	= medium bark	301	349
⊠	= brick	356	5975
✳	= turf	371	854
◺	= medium dark beige	407	914
⟋	= tan	437	362
◗	= medium light teal	598	167
◿	= med. lt. teal/lt. denim	598/3752	167/343
●	= very dark fawn	632	936
∩	= sand	677	886
◥	= medium camel	680	901
·	= very light ecru	712	926
│	= light sand	739	885
�	= light peach	746	275
◖	= med. lt. terra cotta	758	337
△	= teal	807	168
∷	= light linen	822	390
◿	= dark saffron	832	907
◆	= fudge	838	380
/	= copper	945	881
▽	= moss green	3012	843
○	= light moss green	3013	842
▲	= dark tawny	3021	905
◡	= medium light sand	3046	887
◸	= very light turf	3047	852
◡	= light denim	3752	343
◣	= aquamarine	3768	779

Tea Party Sampler

*"Excess of ceremony shews
want of breeding. That civility
is best which excludes all
superfluous formality.
Mary Varick. 1789. New York."*

FRAMED MEASUREMENTS

7 x 12 in. (18 x 31 cm)

EMBROIDERY MEASUREMENTS

4 x 9 in. (10.5 x 23 cm)

MATERIALS

9-3/4 x 15-1/2 in. (25 x 40 cm) of Aida cloth with 14 thread groups per inch (5.5 per cm); embroidery floss as indicated on the key to the chart; if desired, a wooden frame 7 x 12 in. (18 x 31 cm).

DIRECTIONS

Mark the horizontal and vertical center of the Aida cloth with basting thread. Cross-stitch the sampler according to the chart using two strands of floss over one thread group of fabric for each stitch.

KEY TO CHART

Symbol	Color	DMC	Anchor	Symbol	Color	DMC	Anchor
·	= white	white	1	⊠	= orange	742	303
●	= dark red	321	47	✚	= light orange	743	302
◣	= grape	340	118	■	= medium ocean blue	792	177
▲	= salmon	352	9	▣	= medium cobalt	809	130
△	= light salmon	353	6	✖	= dark mint green	911	205
×	= very light lime	369	1043	◆	= light blush	963	73
◙	= dark magenta	602	63	=	= light lime	966	240
❖	= medium magenta	603	62	△	= med. light turquoise	992	186
◈	= light rosebud	604	55	✛	= very light jonquil	3078	292
✖	= medium spring green	703	238	◤	= dark cherry	3705	35
‖	= light jonquil	727	293	▫	= light blueberry	3747	120
⧗	= dark tangerine	740	316				

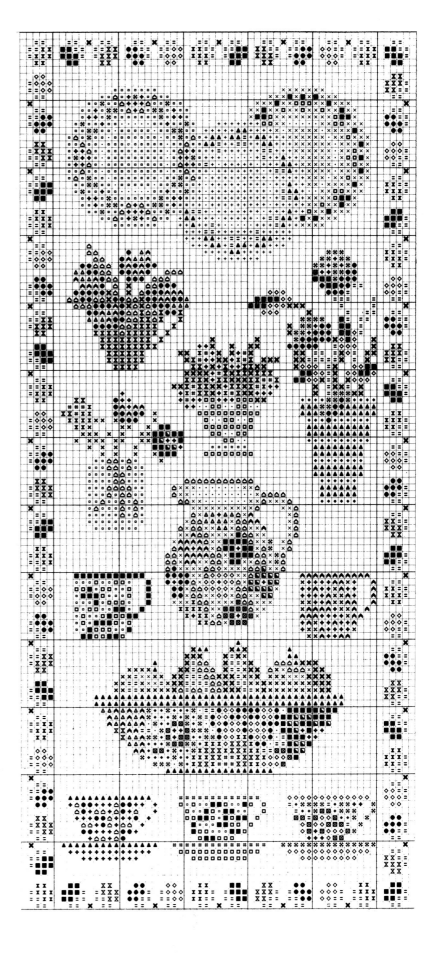

Lilies of the Valley Sampler

FROM MARTHA PERRY'S SAMPLER, ABOUT 1800:

"A blind woman's soliloquy.
Are not the sparrows daily fed by thee,
And will thou clothe the lillies and not me.
Begone distrust! I shall have clothes and bread,
While lillies flourish, and the birds are fed."

FINISHED MEASUREMENTS

10-1/2 x 14-1/2 in. (27 x 37.5 cm)

EMBROIDERY MEASUREMENTS

6 x 9 in. (15 x 23 cm)

MATERIALS

13 x 17 in. (33.5 x 44 cm) of white linen with 35 threads per inch (14 per cm); DMC or Anchor embroidery floss as indicated on the key to the chart plus slate #930 or #1035 and pink #776 or #24; frame (optional).

DIRECTIONS

Mark the center of the fabric with horizontal and vertical basting threads. Position point M at the bottom center. Using two strands of floss over two threads of fabric for each stitch, cross-stitch the motif according to the chart.

Embroider in outline stitch over completed cross-stitch using one strand of floss:

- in and around the bow with pink #776 or #24 and with slate #930 or #1035;
- along the leaves at the upper left with light yellow #445 or #288;
- and all remaining figures in dark mint green #911 or #205.

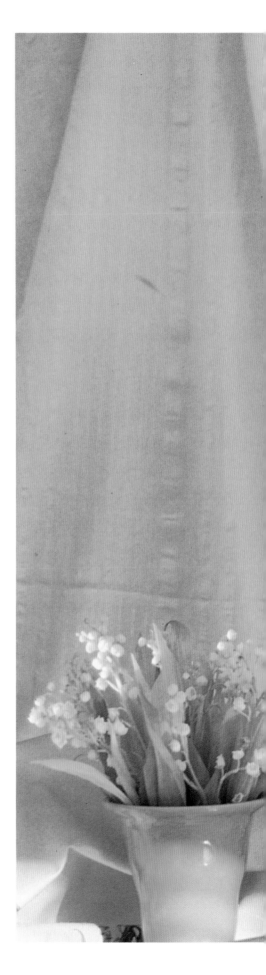

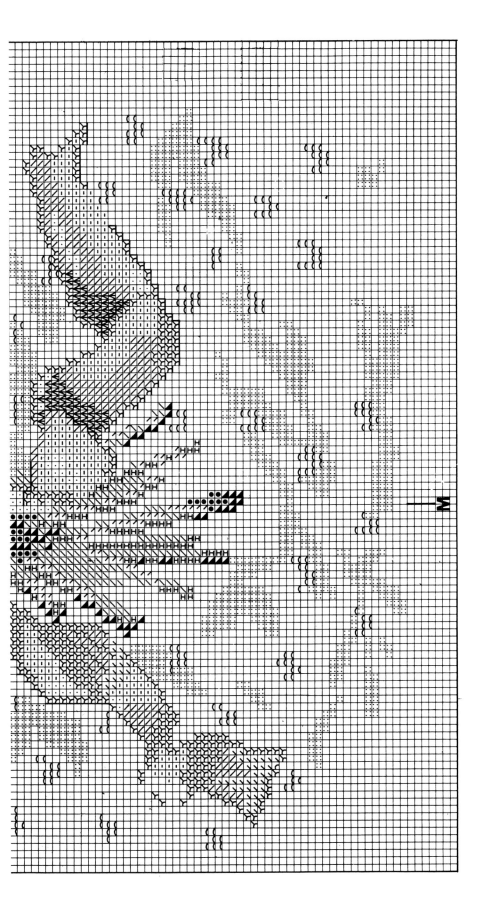

KEY TO CHART

		DMC	Anchor
·	= white	white	1
◖	= light wine	225	892
◺	= very light lime	369	1043
▱	= light yellow	445	288
●	= avocado	469	267
◿	= light azure	519	1038
◣	= dark forest green	561	212
▨	= medium dark olive	581	281
H	= medium spring green	703	238

		DMC	Anchor
∴	= light peach	746	275
▯	= light delft	828	975
◪	= dark mint green	911	205
◠	= medium seafoam	928	274
◹	= very light beige	948	1011
◺	= lime	955	241
◩	= peacock blue	996	433
◿	= very light avocado	3348	264

Brownstone House Sampler

"J. W. & A. PICKET announce to their friends and the public, that they have engaged an Instructress who is well qualified to superintend not only the manners and morals of female pupils, but also their instruction in the various descriptions of needle-work."

—*BALTIMORE AMERICAN AND COMMERCIAL DAILY ADVERTISER,*
SEPTEMBER 1821

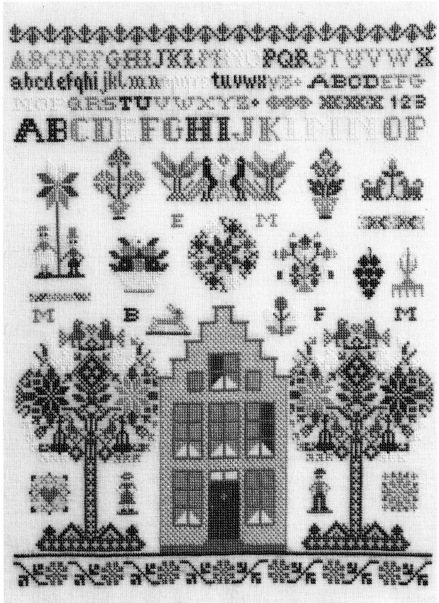

EMBROIDERY MEASUREMENTS

11 x 13-1/2 in. (28 x 35 cm)

MATERIALS

19-1/2 x 21-1/2 in. (50 x 55 cm) of ecru linen with 30 threads per inch (12 per cm); embroidery floss as indicated on the key to the chart; frame, if desired.

DIRECTIONS

Mark the center of the fabric with horizontal and vertical basting threads, then cross-stitch the motifs according to the chart, using two strands of floss over two fabric threads for each stitch.

Embroider the eyes of the figures at the bottom in French knots using two strands of dark mocha floss #433 or #357.

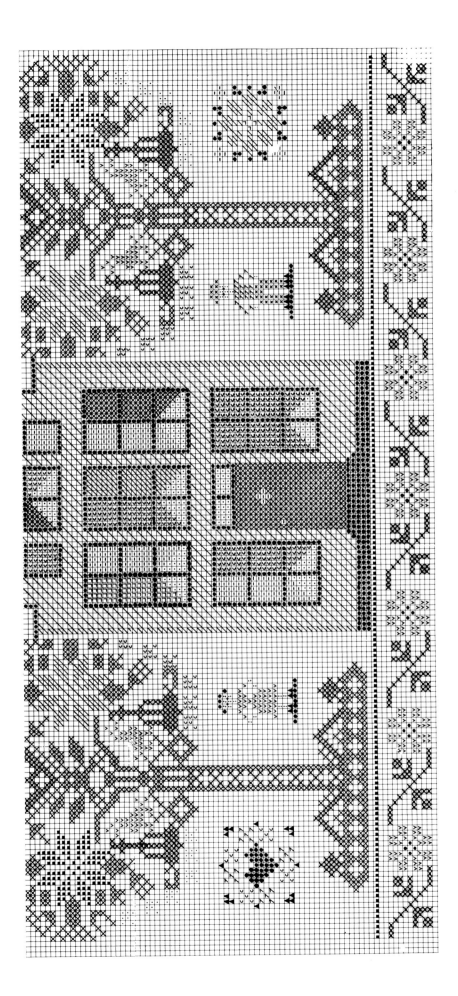

KEY TO CHART

	DMC	Anchor			DMC	Anchor
⊠ = jade	320	215	✕ = teal		807	168
C = light gray	415	398	— = medium glacier blue		827	159
⧄ = medium nutmeg	422	373	■ = light slate		931	1034
◀ = dark mocha	433	357	∨ = dark antique blue		932	1033
● = dark tan	435	365	⟋ = light mint green		954	203
∴ = light sand	739	885	◤ = avocado		3346	267
· = medium peach	744	301	☐ = very light avocado		3348	264

Alpine Flowers Sampler

FROM A SAMPLER BY TWELVE-YEAR-OLD
SARAH ANN BOYER OF COLUMBIA, PENNSYLVANIA:

"Sarah Ann Boyer . . . 1819
Ever charming, ever new
When will the landscape tire
the view"

FINISHED MEASUREMENTS

16-1/2 x 22-3/4 in. (42 x 58.5 cm)

EMBROIDERY MEASUREMENTS

10 x 16-1/2 in. (26 x 42 cm)

MATERIALS

25-1/4 x 31-1/4 in. (65 x 80 cm) of white linen with 28 threads per inch
(11 per cm); DMC or Anchor embroidery floss as indicated on the key
to the chart plus dark gray #414 or #235, coffee #433 or #358, dark olive
green #732 or #281, olive green #734 or #279, dark pine #890 or #879,
medium dark avocado #937 or #268, and light rust #977 or #1002; frame
(optional).

DIRECTIONS

Mark the horizontal and vertical center of the fabric with basting thread,
then cross-stitch according to the chart, using two strands of floss over
two threads of linen for each stitch.

Outline stitch over completed cross-stitch, using one strand of floss.
Outline stitches are indicated by DMC floss number on the chart itself.
For example, outline the leaves of the alpine aster with medium lime,
DMC #989 (Anchor #242); outline the centers of the edelweiss with coffee, DMC #433 (Anchor #358), and the edelweiss flower petals with
olive green, DMC #734 (Anchor #279). Outlines are not called for on all
flowers.

The number at the lower right of the square around each flower indicates
the DMC floss number to use for embroidering the square in outline
stitch, using one strand of floss. For example, outline the square around
the anemone in medium light green, DMC #987 (Anchor #244), and the
square around the silver thistle in dark pine, DMC #890 (Anchor #879).

KEY TO CHART

	DMC	Anchor
· = white	white	1
∨ = jade	320	215
◆ = red	321	9046
∅ = medium dark salmon	350	11
S = brick	356	3975
‖ = medium dark beige	407	914
∅ = brown	434	370
∧ = tan	437	362
∕ = medium yellow	444	290
∣ = light yellow	445	288
+ = chartreuse	471	255
− = light chartreuse	472	253
■ = medium dark pine	501	878
E = medium pine	502	877
L = light pine	503	875
◣ = sapphire	517	162
◤ = dark violet	550	101
⬡ = light violet	553	98
N = lilac	554	96
● = medium forest green	562	210
∨ = medium light teal	598	167
● = light emerald	700	228
Z = medium spring green	703	238
X = light parrot green	704	256
∴ = medium light jonquil	726	295
□ = medium olive green	733	280
◿ = dark orange	741	304
⬔ = light orange	743	302
▬ = dark topaz	781	309
∕ = very light pink	819	271
∖ = medium glacier blue	827	159
∷ = dark saffron	833	907
∕ = dark coffee	839	360
⊙ = fuchsia	893	28
◹ = dark pink	894	26
⊠ = dark chartreuse	907	255
O = medium turquoise	958	187
△ = medium rust	976	1001
▲ = medium light green	987	244
∙ and ◤ = light green	988	243
⊟ = medium lime	989	242

traveler's joy (old man's beard)

alpine aster

Dusty Miller

pillow plant

alpine primrose

spiderweb leek

KEY TO CHART

	DMC	Anchor
◗ = amethyst	3042	870
◺ = medium light orchid	3608	86
M = med. light raspberry	3687	68
◖ = very light cherry	3708	31

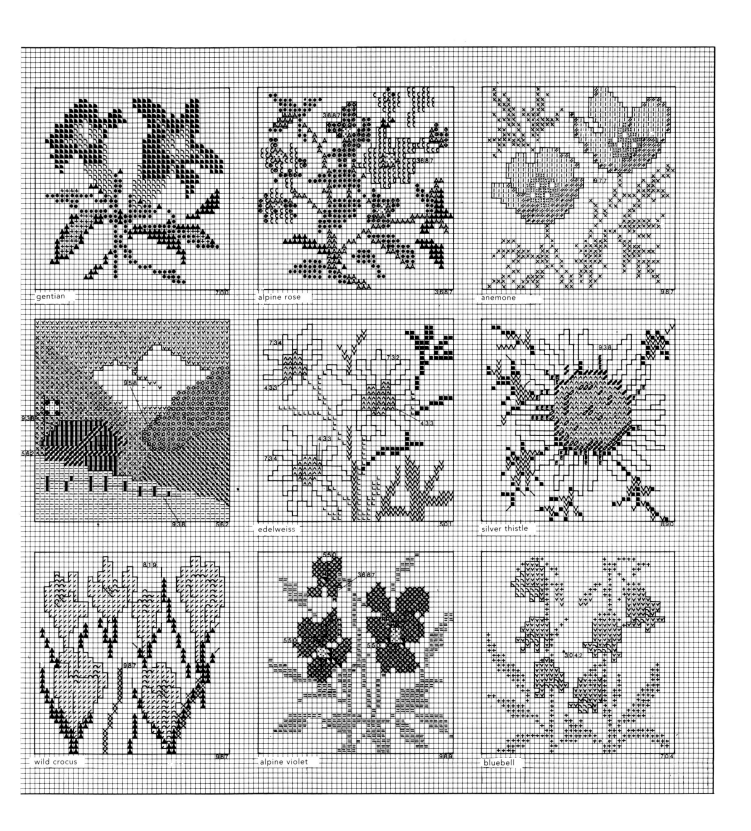

gentian   700

alpine rose   3687

anemone   987

edelweiss   501

silver thistle   890

wild crocus   987

alpine violet   989

bluebell   704

Iris Sampler

"Let the bright rosy morning
Call me forth to take the air
Cheerful spring with smiles returning
Ushers in the newborn year…
Wrought By Lucy D. Stickney
Charlestown November 18 1830 Aged 12"

KEY TO CHART

		DMC	Anchor
	= light purple	208	110
	= dark lavender	209	109
	= lavender	211	342
	= grape	340	118
	= brown	434	370
	= light toast	436	1045
	= dark chartreuse	471	255
	= light chartreuse	472	253
	= medium pine	502	877
	= violet	552	99
	= lilac	554	96
	= dark forest green	561	212
	= medium forest green	562	210
	= med. lt. forest green	563	208
	= very dark fawn	632	936
	= dark linen	640	393
	= medium linen	642	392
	= camel	676	891
	= emerald	702	239
	= medium spring green	703	238
	= light jonquil	727	293
	= light camel	729	890
	= light loden green	772	259
	= topaz	783	307
	= dark blue gray	792	941
	= ocean blue	793	176
	= light ocean blue	794	175
	= dark chartreuse	907	255
	= terra cotta	921	338
	= dark aquamarine	924	851
	= med. lt. aquamarine	926	850
	= light green	988	243
	= medium lime	989	242
	= medium copper	3064	883
	= very light jonquil	3078	292
	= medium coral	3328	1024
	= avocado	3346	267
	= very light avocado	3348	264

FINISHED MEASUREMENTS

15-1/2 x 20 in. (39.5 x 51.5 cm)

EMBROIDERY MEASUREMENTS

10-1/2 x 14-3/4 in. (27 x 38 cm)

MATERIALS

23-1/2 x 27-1/4 in. (60 x 70 cm) of ecru linen with 25 threads per inch (10 per cm); embroidery floss as indicated on the key to the chart plus dark mint green #911 or #205 and dark rust #922 or #1003; frame, if desired.

DIRECTIONS

Mark the horizontal and vertical center of the fabric with basting thread, then cross-stitch the motif according to the chart. Work each cross-stitch using two strands of floss over two fabric threads.

Embroider in outline stitch over completed cross-stitch using two strands of floss:

- around the long leaf to the right of the iris bulb with dark mint green #911 or #205;
- around the yellow brown leaves above the large bulb with dark rust #922 or #1003;
- and around all remaining figures in the same color as the cross-stitching or one shade darker.

Embroider the words in stem stitch using two strands of grape floss #340 or #118.

Field Flowers Sampler

"In a dull company and in dull weather…it is ill manners to read; it is ill manners to leave them; no card playing there among genteel people…. The needle is then a valuable resource."

—THOMAS JEFFERSON TO HIS DAUGHTER MARTHA, 1787

FINISHED MEASUREMENTS

19-1/2 x 24-1/2 in. (50 x 63 cm)

EMBROIDERY MEASUREMENTS

15-1/2 x 21 in. (40 x 54 cm)

MATERIALS

29-1/4 x 33 in. (75 x 85 cm) of linen with 25 threads per inch (10 per cm); embroidery floss as indicated on the key to the chart; frame (optional).

DIRECTIONS

Mark the horizontal and vertical center of the fabric with basting thread, then embroider in cross-stitch following the chart, using two strands of floss over two threads of fabric for each stitch. Where two color numbers are given, use one strand of each color.

Embroider in outline stitch over completed cross-stitch. Use one strand of floss in and around the leaves. For all remaining outline stitches, use two strands of floss to stitch:

- in and around the stems of the blue cornflowers with medium camel #680 or #901;
- around the camel-colored petals of the poppies with medium salmon #351 or #10;
- the antennas of the butterflies and in and around the white flowers with gray #318 or #399;
- in the lower left flower with medium watermelon #335 or #38;
- around the yellow flowers with very light jonquil #3078 or #292;
- the beetle's antenna and legs with dark charcoal #413 or #401;
- and all other outline stitches in the same color as the cross-stitching or a shade darker.

KEY TO CHART

		DMC	Anchor
·	= white	white	1
◹	= light wine	225	892
◥	= dark bark	300	352
◸	= yellow	307	289
◪	= dark mauve	315	1019
∟	= medium mauve	316	1017
◹	= gray	318	399
⊠	= dark grape	333	119
◗	= med. watermelon pink	335	38
∷	= grape	340	118
◣	= light red	349	46
⊠	= medium dark salmon	350	11
⊤	= medium salmon	351	10
−	= light salmon	353	6
⋰	= brick	356	5975
⊠	= brick/moss green	356/3012	5975/843
■	= juniper	367	217
◤	= dark charcoal	413	401
◹	= dark yellow	444	291
◿	= light yellow	445	288
◺	= avocado	469	267
◹	= light parrot green	470	256
◺	= medium light avocado	471	266
◺	= light chartreuse	472	253
▼	= medium dark pine	501	878
⊠	= medium pine	502	877
▽	= light pine	503	875
◣	= dark forest green	561	212
◺	= camel	676	891
⋰	= sand	677	886
◠	= medium camel	680	901
◠	= medium spring green	704	238
⋱	= very light ecru	712	926
◿	= medium apricot	721	324
◖	= light topaz	725	305
◹	= orange	742	303

		DMC	Anchor
•	= very dark blue gray	792	941
◹	= light ocean blue	794	175
◹	= light sapphire	813	161
◢	= dark salmon	817	13
■	= dark blue black	823	127
◿	= sapphire	826	162
◹	= dark saffron	833	907
⫽	= medium saffron	834	874
✳	= dark nutmeg	869	375
⊞	= dark nutmeg/med. rust	869/976	375/1001
◹	= parrot green	906	257
◹	= dark chartreuse	907	255
◹	= dark mint green	911	205
▲	= slate	930	1035
◹	= light blush	963	73
◗	= medium rust	976	1001
∷	= light rust	977	1002
◥	= dark green	986	246
●	= medium light green	987	244
⋰	= light green	988	243
◹	= medium lime	989	242
⊙	= dark moss green	3011	846
◿	= moss green	3012	843
◺	= med. light amethyst	3041	871
○	= medium copper	3064	883
◗	= very light jonquil	3078	292
C	= light watermelon pink	3326	36
◹	= medium coral	3328	1024
◢	= medium melon	3340	329
◹	= light melon	3341	328
◥	= medium dark avocado	3345	268
⋱	= medium loden green	3346	262
◹	= very light avocado	3348	264
⊹	= med. light raspberry	3687	68
◹	= light raspberry	3688	66
◹	= very light cherry	3708	31

Spring Birds Samplers

FROM A SAMPLER BY HANNAH WOLCOTT, WOLCOTT, MASSACHUSETTS, AGE FIFTEEN, ABOUT 1800:

"Hannah S Wolcott
On Music
Music the fiercest grief can charm
And fates severest rage disarm
Music can soften pain to ease
And make despair and madness please"

FINISHED MEASUREMENTS

About 8 in. (21 cm) each, in diameter

EMBROIDERY MEASUREMENTS

4-3/4 x 6-1/2 in. (12 x 17 cm) each

MATERIALS

For each sampler, 13-1/2 x 13-1/2 in. (35 x 35 cm) of linen with 35 threads per inch (14 per cm); embroidery floss as indicated on the key to the chart; a round frame, if desired.

DIRECTIONS

Mark the horizontal and vertical center of the fabric with basting thread, then embroider the motif in cross-stitch, using two strands of floss over two fabric threads for each stitch.

Using one strand of floss, embroider in outline stitch over finished cross-stitch in the same color as the cross-stitch or a shade darker.

KEY TO CHART   ENGLISH ROBIN

		DMC	Anchor
●	= gray	318	399
□	= medium dark salmon	350	11
=	= medium salmon	351	10
.•	= very light lime	369	1043
H	= brown	434	370
Z	= toast	435	1046
C	= light toast	436	1045
+	= tan	437	362
\	= light fog	453	231
▼	= avocado	469	267
◣	= light chartreuse	472	253
⊠	= light red orange	608	332
O	= dark tangerine	740	316
∷	= orange	742	303
−	= medium peach	744	301
⏽	= light cocoa	754	1012
•	= silver	762	234
■	= dark coffee	839	360
ø	= dark fawn	840	379
◤	= dark green	986	246
⊓	= light green	988	243
∨	= medium lime	989	242
∟	= very light avocado	3348	264

KEY TO CHART

GOLDFINCH

		DMC	Anchor				DMC	Anchor
•	= white	white	2	‖	= medium desert		612	832
■	= black	310	403	H	= medium camel		680	901
◻	= gray	318	399	/	= silver		762	234
O	= medium salmon	351	10	◿	= light sapphire		813	161
∷	= light salmon	353	6	▼	= dark sapphire		824	164
⊓	= dark charcoal	413	401	◻	= sapphire		826	162
◻	= light toast	436	1045	∴	= light delft		828	975
●	= dark fog	451	233	—	= very light beige		948	1011
Z	= fog	452	232	∨	= medium light sand		3046	887
Z	= light fog	453	231	∅	= medium light avocado	3347	266
⊠	= medium dark sand	610	889	L	= very light avocado		3348	264

114

Wildflowers Sampler

FROM A 1789 SAMPLER BY ELIZABETH RAYMOND:

"Lord give me wisdom to direct my ways
I beg not riches nor yet length of days
My life is a flower, the time it hath to last
Is mixed with frost and shook
with every blast."

FINISHED MEASUREMENTS

17-3/4 x 23-1/2 in. (45.5 x 60 cm)

EMBROIDERY MEASUREMENTS

15-1/2 x 21 in. (40 x 54 cm)

MATERIALS

25-1/4 x 31-1/4 in. (65 x 80 cm) of ecru linen with 26 or 27 threads per inch (10 or 11 per cm); embroidery floss as indicated on the key to the chart; frame (optional).

DIRECTIONS

Mark the center of the fabric with horizontal and vertical basting threads, then cross-stitch the motifs according to the chart. Use two strands of floss over two fabric threads for each stitch.

Embroider in outline stitch over completed cross-stitch, according to the Anchor floss number on the chart; use one or two strands as indicated with the floss number. For instance, the number 039 to the left of the fern at lower left directs you to outline stitch with one strand of dark watermelon (Anchor #39 or DMC #309); the number 371(2) to the right of the fern tells you to outline stitch with two strands of dark brown (Anchor #371 or DMC #433).

KEY TO CHART

	Anchor	DMC	
·	1	white	= white
−	8	353	= medium light salmon
/	33	3706	= light cherry
◣	39	309	= dark watermelon pink
◇	49	3689	= light blossom pink
⊡	50	957	= blossom pink
◔	52	899	= medium blossom pink
◑	57	601	= medium rosebud pink
⌣	108	210	= light lavender

	Anchor	DMC	
⊡	110	208	= light purple
⊙	117	341	= light grape
⊳	118	340	= grape
◀	119	333	= dark grape
∷	213	504	= light jade
∩	240	966	= light lime
⊠	242	989	= medium lime
◣	243	988	= light green
◤	244	987	= medium light green

	Anchor	DMC	
⊘	254	907	= chartreuse
⟋	255	471	= light chartreuse
⟋	256	906	= light parrot green
●	258	904	= dark parrot green
⟍	265	3348	= very light avocado
◀	268	937	= medium dark avocado
=	280	733	= medium olive green
⊠	295	726	= medium light jonquil
+	300	745	= peach

	Anchor	DMC	
⊔	301	744	= medium peach
Z	302	743	= light orange
O	368	945	= dark spice
X	369	435	= light brown
◪	371	433	= dark brown
⊡	372	738	= light nutmeg
▼	375	869	= dark nutmeg
⊡	906	829	= dark camel

Bellflower

Speedwell

White Windflower

Lily of the Valley

Solomon's Seal

Dandelion

Slender Cowslip

(Wild)
Wood Strawberry

Ivy

Wood
Violet

Periwinkle

Plantain

Daisy

Rosehip

Lesser Celandine

Foxglove

Male Fern

Garden Sampler Trio

"Keep clean your samplers, sleepe not as you sit
For sluggishness doth spoile the rarest wit."

—*A BOOK OF CURIOUS AND STRANGE INVENTIONS CALLED THE FIRST PART OF NEEDLEWORKES*, 1596

FINISHED MEASUREMENTS

12-3/4 x 12-3/4 in. (33 x 33 cm) each

EMBROIDERY MEASUREMENTS

9 x 9 in. (23 x 23 cm) each

MATERIALS

For the 3 samplers: 1/2 yd. (.45 m) of linen 62-1/2 in. (160 cm) wide with 28 threads per inch (11 per cm); embroidery floss as indicated in the keys to the charts plus green #986 or #245.

DIRECTIONS

For one sampler, cut a square of linen 17-1/2 x 17-1/2 in. (45 x 45 cm). Mark the horizontal and vertical center of the fabric with basting thread. Cross-stitch the motif according to the chart using two strands of floss over two threads of fabric for each stitch.

Outline stitch over completed cross-stitch using two strands of floss unless otherwise indicated.

For the quotation sampler, outline stitch the letters and stem stitch the tendrils between the leaves with medium light avocado #3347 or #266 and outline stitch the remaining figures with one strand of green #986 or #245.

For the watering can sampler, outline stitch:
- around the leaves in the corners with light emerald #700 or #228;

- in and around the two flower pots with dark coffee #898 or #360;
- and all remaining figures with light charcoal #317 or #400.

For the flower pots sampler, outline stitch:
- in and around the medium mocha flower pot saucer and the large flower pot with one strand of black #310 or #403;
- in and around the two small flower pots with medium terra cotta #920 or #339;
- and all other elements with dark juniper #319 or #218.

Stem stitch the scrolls in the border with two strands of medium light forest green #563 or #208.

KEY TO CHART WATERING CAN

		DMC	Anchor
⋅	= white	white	1
■	= light charcoal	317	400
◺	= gray	318	399
○	= delft	334	977
●	= juniper	367	216
╱	= medium jade	368	214
⋰	= light toast	436	347
⊤	= chartreuse	471	265
⌣	= light chartreuse	472	253
∷	= light jade	504	213
▲	= light emerald	700	228
╱	= very light ecru	712	926
⌐	= medium light jonquil	726	295
◣	= dark coffee	898	360
◿	= dark mint green	911	205
◢	= medium terra cotta	920	339
⊟	= light copper	951	880
◺	= light lime	966	240
✳	= medium mocha	975	355
◜	= light silver	3024	397
⊠	= med. light avocado	3347	266
◺	= light brick	3778	337
◠	= medium beige	3779	336
◉	= charcoal	3799	236

QUOTATION

	DMC	Anchor
● = juniper	367	216
◿ = medium jade	368	214
◹ = light chartreuse	472	253
· = light jade	504	213
◥ = medium mint green	913	204
◺ = light green	988	243
⊠ = med. light avocado	3347	266
◖ = very light avocado	3348	264

KEY TO CHART **FLOWER POTS**

	DMC	Anchor
◐ = black	310	403
◣ = light charcoal	317	400
⬙ = gray	318	399
■ = dark juniper	319	218
○ = delft	334	977
◺ = light toast	436	347
● = avocado	469	267
⊤ = chartreuse	471	265
◡ = light chartreuse	472	253
◿ = med. lt. forest green	563	208
▲ = light emerald	700	228
◠ = medium light jonquil	726	295
· = light orange	743	311
◣ = dark coffee	898	360
◹ = dark mint green	911	205
◗ = medium terra cotta	920	339
◹ = light mint green	954	225
◺ = medium mocha	975	355
◹ = light rust	977	313
⣿ = light silver	3024	397
⊠ = med. light avocado	3347	266
◖ = very light avocado	3348	264
◺ = light brick	3778	337
— = medium beige	3779	336

Sunflowers Sampler

"Three Golden Rules
Worthy the observation of every one
Do everything in its proper time
keep everything to its proper use
Put everything in its proper place
Elizabeth Dore Aged 13
Portsmouth May 31 A.D. 1822"

FINISHED MEASUREMENTS

20-1/4 x 35 in. (52 x 90 cm)

MATERIALS

25-1/4 x 40 in. (65 x 103 cm) of white linen with 20 threads per inch (8 per cm); white sewing machine thread; Lingarn (or its equivalent) or DMC or Anchor embroidery floss as indicated on the key to the chart plus blossom pink #326 or #59, dark forest green #561 or #212, light red #666 or #46, medium spring green #703 or #238, dark coffee #839 or #360, medium light green #987 or #244, and medium melon #3340 or #329.

DIRECTIONS

Mark the center of the fabric with horizontal and vertical basting threads, then cross-stitch the motif according to the chart, using one strand of Lingarn or four strands of embroidery floss over two threads of linen for each stitch.

Embroider in outline stitch over completed cross-stitch using two strands of floss. Use dark tangerine (Lingarn #595, DMC #970, or Anchor #316) to outline the sunflower leaves, the stems of the reddish-orange flowers, and a few of the leaves at the bottom of the picture. For all other outlining, use a color that matches the cross-stitches or a shade darker.

FINISHING

For the openwork border, draw four fabric threads toward the corners, as follows:

- on the bottom and the left side, begin 23 fabric threads from the outermost cross-stitch;

- on the top, begin 33 fabric threads from the top-most cross-stitch;
- on the right side, begin 19 fabric threads from the outermost cross-stitch.

Leaving little end-pieces of thread sticking out at the corners, trim the fabric to 2-1/4 in. (6 cm) from the openwork border. Baste a 3/4 in. (2 cm) hem, with another 3/4 in. (3 cm) turned under, all the way around the piece. Finish the corners diagonally.

Fasten the hem with ladder hemstitches (see the Appendix) over four fabric threads. Weave the end-pieces back into the fabric.

Design Note: The sampler in the photo is embroidered with Lingarn, a very fine, tough, two-ply yarn or linen thread.

KEY TO CHART

Symbol		DMC	Anchor	Lingarn
·	= white	white	1	600
✖	= dark rose	309	42	572
	= med. watermelon	335	38	573
●	= light red	349	46	539
◖	= coffee	433	358	594
Z	= chartreuse	471	255	625
●	= red orange	606	334	634
⊠	= light parrot green	704	256	591
		= med. light jonquil	726	295	504
◁	= orange	742	303	596
◿	= very lt. loden green	772	259	653
▷	= topaz	783	307	660
■	= dark carmine	814	45	637
—	= light pink	818	23	532
▱	= medium saffron	834	874	506
⋅	= dark tangerine	970	316	595
○	= very light jonquil	3078	292	666
▶	= light watermelon	3326	36	576
◣	= med. dark avocado	3345	268	627
◪	= med. light avocado	3347	266	589
	= very light avocado	3348	264	592

Romantic Age Sampler

FROM A NEW ENGLAND SAMPLER:

"O hills O vales whare I have strayd
O woods that rapt me in your shade
O scenes that I have wandered over
O scenes I shall behold no more
I take a Longe Last Lingering view
Adieu my native Land adieu
Elizabeth Brown's Work 1834"

EMBROIDERY MEASUREMENTS

18 x 21-3/4 in. (46.5 x 56 cm)

MATERIALS

25-1/4 x 29-1/4 in. (65 x 75 cm) of ecru linen with 25 threads per inch (10 threads per cm); embroidery floss or DMC crewel wool (or its equivalent) as indicated on the key to the chart; frame (optional).

DIRECTIONS

Mark the horizontal and vertical center of the fabric with basting thread and cross-stitch the motif according to the chart. Use two strands of embroidery floss or one strand of crewel wool over two fabric threads for each stitch. (The chart shows half of the flower border; turn the chart upside down and repeat this motif for the top of the sampler.)

Design Note: In the wreaths at the top of the sampler, the initials in the middle are the embroiderer's and those at the left and right are her parents'. These traditional designs are drawn from a German book of pattern samples and are also called "Berlin work." The sampler in the photograph is embroidered in wool on linen.

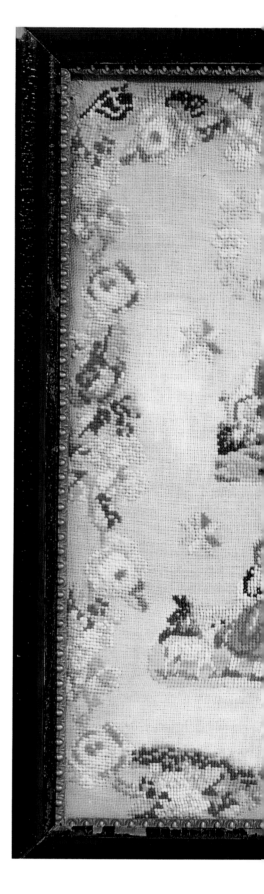

KEY TO CHART

		DMC Wool	DMC Floss	Anchor Floss
⌐	= very light beige	8101A	948	1011
●	= dark cherry	8102	498	1005
⊠	= very dark wine	8106	221	897
○	= wine	8107	224	893
◣	= medium copper	8108	3064	883
◣	= slate	8202	930	1035
⊙	= med. lt. aquamarine	8203	926	850
⊓	= dark seafoam	8204	927	848
⌐	= medium seafoam	8204A	928	274
⌐	= light cobalt	8210	775	128
⊠	= medium bark	8301	301	349
+	= light camel	8303A	729	890
◺	= medium harvest	8305	834	945
▼	= medium coffee	8306	801	359
◿	= dark fawn	8307	840	379
◹	= medium tawny	8308	3032	903
■	= medium gray green	8309	935	861
⋀	= nutmeg	8321	420	374
⊤	= light tan	8322	738	361
⊠	= medium camel	8324	680	901
∷	= sand	8327	677	886
▲	= dark gray green	8404	520	862
=	= med. lt. loden green	8405	3053	261
×	= moss green	8412	3012	843
╱	= dark moss green	8412A	3011	846
◢	= dark pine	8416	500	879
⌐	= tan	8501	437	362
·	= ecru	8502A	ecru	387
∨	= medium nutmeg	8503	422	373
⊺	= medium wheat	8504	422	943
╱	= copper	8504A	945	881
◖	= dark blue black	navy	823	127

Roses Sampler

"While on my varied hues you gaze
And fancy beauty glowing there
Reflect! All beauty is but nought
Tis virtue that adorns the fair
M. Witmer
Philadela
Wrought 1828"

FINISHED MEASUREMENTS

17-3/4 x 21-3/4 in. (45.5 x 56 cm)

EMBROIDERY MEASUREMENTS

15-1/4 x 19-1/2 in. (39 x 50 cm)

MATERIALS

25-1/4 x 29-1/4 in. (65 x 75 cm) of white linen with 25 threads per inch (10 threads per cm); DMC or Anchor embroidery floss as indicated on the key to the chart plus medium coral #3328 or #1024 and medium light coral #760 or #1022; frame (optional).

DIRECTIONS

Mark the horizontal and vertical center of the fabric with basting thread, then work each cross-stitch with two strands of floss over two threads of fabric, according to the chart.

Use one strand of floss to embroider in outline stitch over completed cross-stitch in the same shade as the cross-stitching or a shade darker, unless a DMC floss number on the chart indicates otherwise. For instance, on Joanna Hill, outline stitch inside the large rose in medium rust (DMC #976 or Anchor #1001) and around the small rose in salmon (DMC #352 or Anchor #9).

Use one strand of floss to embroider the names of the roses in petit point (see the Appendix) using two strands of medium coral #3328 or #1024 over one fabric thread on the front of the work, and over two fabric threads on the back.

FINISHING

Use a drawn-thread technique for the openwork borders, whose locations are shown on the chart: for the outside border, draw two fabric threads out of the fabric, beginning and ending 1-1/2 in. (4 cm) from each corner and leaving 2 in. (5 cm) of uncut thread at each corner. Secure the remaining thread ends on the back of the fabric by weaving them back into the fabric for a few stitches, then snipping off the ends. For the inner borders around each rose, draw one fabric thread out of the fabric, then secure the thread ends in the same way.

Finish the drawn-thread borders with a ladder hemstitch (see the Appendix), using one strand of medium light coral #760 or #1022 over three fabric threads.

KEY TO CHART

Symbol	Color	DMC	Anchor		Symbol	Color	DMC	Anchor
•	= white	white	1		o	= orange	742	303
◪	= light purple	208	110		∴	= light orange	743	302
▷	= dark lavender	209	109		⊥	= medium peach	744	301
⌐	= lavender	211	342				= peach	745	300
N	= med. watermelon pink	335	38		∴	= light peach	746	275
⊂	= light grape	341	117		∙∙	= light glacier blue	747	158
●	= medium dark salmon	350	11		∷	= light coral	761	1021
∙	= medium salmon	351	10		∙	= silver	762	234
△	= salmon	352	9		—	= very lt. loden green	772	259
∴	= light salmon	353	6		⌐	= pink	776	24
◣	= juniper	367	217		▶	= dark salmon	817	13
∨	= medium jade	368	214		⁄	= light pink	818	23
⁄	= very light lime	369	1043		⟍	= very light pink	819	271
Z	= brown	434	370		⊠	= medium glacier blue	827	159
⊘	= dark chartreuse	471	255		■	= dark maroon	915	1029
●	= medium rosebud pink	601	57		⟍	= very light beige	948	1011
⊘	= dark magenta	602	63		⌐	= medium light beige	950	4146
∧	= medium magenta	603	62		◥	= dark blush	962	75
+	= light rosebud pink	604	55		⋉	= light blush	963	73
⬜	= blossom pink	605	50		∨	= medium rust	976	1001
▼	= very dark fawn	632	936		⊤	= light rust	977	1002
⁄	= camel	676	891		⊠	= medium lime	989	242
S	= medium camel	680	901		H	= light watermelon pink	3326	36
⊠	= medium dark orchid	718	88		◣	= med. dark loden green	3363	262
⊃	= light camel	729	890		=	= light loden green	3364	260
‖	= olive green	734	279		◪	= light cherry	3706	33

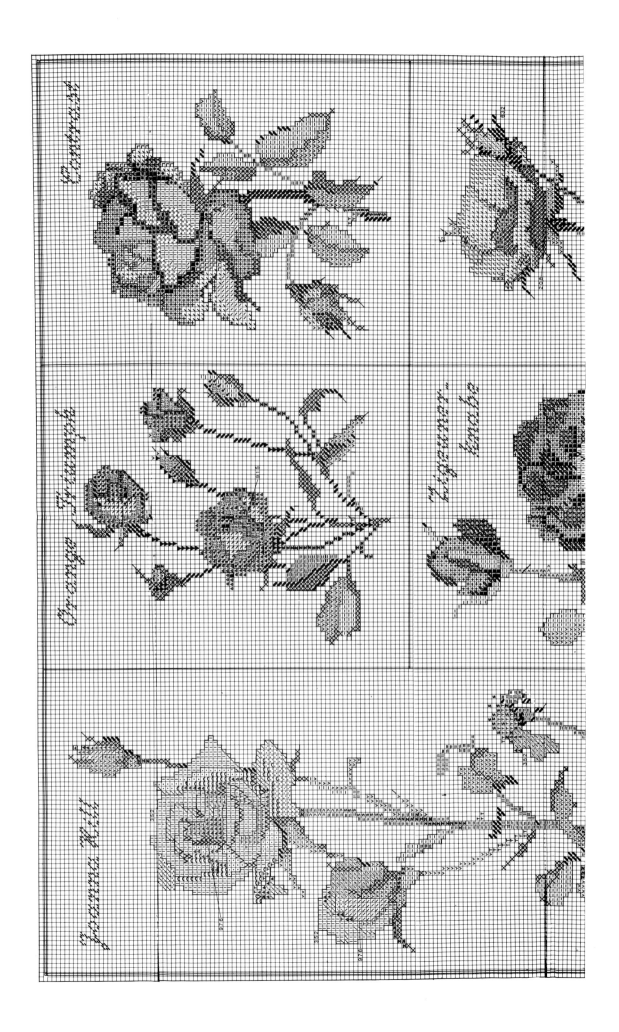

Cottage Garden Sampler

"Now when she had dined, then she might go to seke out her examplers…and to sitte her donne and take it forthe by little and little, and thus with her needle to passe the after noone with devising of things for her owne wearygne."

—BARNABE RICH, *OF PHYLOTUS AND EMILIA,* 1581

FINISHED MEASUREMENTS

Spring: 9-1/4 x 20-3/4 in. (24 x 53 cm)

Winter: 9-1/4 x 10 in. (24 x 26 cm)

Note: The spring scene is framed as a three-paneled, hinged picture. The two parts of the winter picture are framed on the backs of the two side panels. When the side panels are folded closed (in toward the center), they cover the central spring landscape and form the winter picture. You thus have the option of stitching the spring picture only.

MATERIALS

1/2 yd. (.4 m) of white linen 63 in. (160 cm) wide with 28 threads per inch (11 per cm); DMC or Anchor embroidery floss as indicated on the key to the chart plus medium forest green #562 or #210 and light emerald #700 or #228; if desired, one frame 9-1/4 x 10 in. (24 x 26 cm), two frames 5 x 9-1/4 in. (13 x 24 cm), and four hinges.

DIRECTIONS

Cut the linen into four pieces 9-3/4 x 15-1/2 in. (25 x 40 cm) and one piece 15-1/2 x 15-1/2 in. (40 x 40 cm). Mark the horizontal and vertical center of each section of the sampler, and cross-stitch the scenes according to the charts. Use two strands of floss over two threads of linen for each stitch, except for the sky, which calls for one strand of floss over two threads of linen for each stitch.

Where the key to the chart lists two color numbers, use one strand of each color.

Embroider in outline stitch over completed cross-stitch using two strands of floss. **For the spring picture:**

- inside the windows with light peach #746 or #275;
- around the windows with light navy #797 or #132;
- around the pink flowers with very light cherry #3708 or #31;
- around the leaves and flowers with light emerald #700 or #228;
- in and around the flower pots with cinnamon #301 or #1049;
- around the watering can with black #310 or #403;
- and around the white, light peach, and medium light orchid flowers with medium forest green #562 or #210.

KEY TO CHART

		DMC	Anchor
· = white		white	1
⊞ = cinnamon		301	1049
■ = black		310	403
◣ = gray		318	399
⌐ = medium jade		368	214
⌐ = very light lime		369	1043
⟋ = light cinnamon		402	1047
▲ = dark gray		414	235
⬓ = light chartreuse		472	253
⌐ = light azure		519	1038
⬔ = light forest green		564	206

		DMC	Anchor
◯ = blossom pink		605	334
C = very light desert		644	830
⌄ = medium light pewter		647	1040
⟍ = light pewter		648	900
● = dark bottle green		701	227
⟋ = medium spring green		703	238
⟍ = light parrot green		704	256
⬓ = light apricot/copper		722/945	323/881
⬓ = light tan/light sand		738/739	361/885
⬓ = light peach		746	275
⬓ = silver		762	234

	DMC	Anchor		DMC	Anchor
⁄ = very light loden green	772	259	◥ = light mint green	954	203
⊡ = pink	776	24	◠ = lime	955	241
■ = light navy	797	132	⁄ = light blush	963	73
◥ = light wedgwood blue	799	136	Z = light rust	977	1002
∩ = light indigo	800	144	▲ = medium light green	987	244
◺ = medium cobalt	809	130	⊠ = light green	988	243
◷ = very light pink	819	271	◫ = medium lime	989	242
− = light delft	828	975	⟋ = medium light avocado	3347	266
◤ = medium red orange	900	333	◳ = very light avocado	3348	264
◺ = medium mint green	913	204	✳ = medium light orchid	3608	86
◺ = dark rust	922	1003	◣ = very light cherry	3708	31

For the winter picture, outline stitch:
- inside the windows with light peach #746 or #275;
- around the windows with light navy #797 or #132;
- in and around the flower pots with brick #356 or #5975;
- and around all remaining features with dark gray #414 or #235.

		DMC	Anchor			DMC	Anchor
⊡	= white	white	1	◹	= medium light copper	758	882
■	= black	310	403	⊡	= silver	762	234
◢	= gray	318	399	╱	= light cobalt	775	128
◪	= brick	356	5975	⊡	= medium light topaz	783	306
▲	= dark gray	414	235	■	= light navy	797	132
◖	= light fog	453	231	◗	= light wedgwood blue	799	136
◣	= very dark fawn	632	936	◸	= medium cobalt	809	130
∴	= light tan/light sand	738/739	361/885	◩	= medium light green	987	244
∵	= light peach	746	275	◫	= medium lime	989	242
⊤	= light cocoa	754	1012	⊟	= cobalt	3325	129

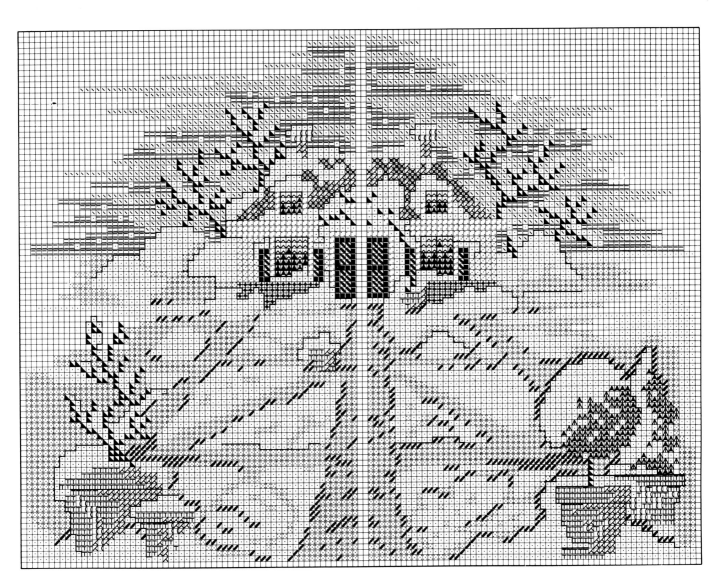

Stitches

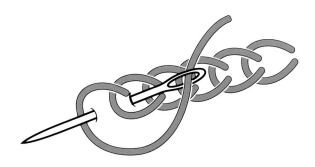

Chain Stitch

Stitched along a marked or imaginary line on your fabric, chain stitches are used for both filling and outlining. Bring the needle to the right side of your work along the line and hold the thread there with your thumb. Poke the needle back through the fabric very close to the same spot, then bring its point up a short distance along the line, looping the thread under the tip of the needle. Pull the thread through.

Repeat the stitch along the line, being sure to take the needle to the inside of the last loop each time you begin a new stitch. To finish a line of chain stitching, bring the needle through to the wrong side of the fabric on the outside of the loop.

Daisy Stitch

This single chain stitch is often used for flower petals. Use the same looping method as for chain stitch, but rather than working along a line, on the second stitch bring your needle to the right side of your work at the base of the next flower petal and continue by making a new stitch for each petal.

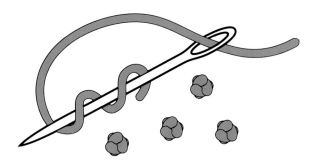

French Knot

The stitch of choice for eyes or flower centers, French knots add depth to your work. On the right side of your piece, wrap the thread twice around the point of the your needle, pull it tight, and insert the needle next to where it came out. Pull the excess thread through, at the same time holding the wrapped thread taut around the needle to form a clean knot. To make a larger knot, wrap the thread more times around the needle.

Stitches

Hemstitch and Ladder Hemstitch

A decorative stitch that is simpler than it looks, hemstitch or ladder hemstitch adds a special touch to an embroidered piece. Worked over an even number of threads (the project directions tell you how many), it gathers or circles thread groups for an openwork effect. For hemstitch, working from left to right on the right side of your work, bring your needle up from the wrong side two fabric threads down from the row you want to stitch. Slip it behind the first thread group from right to left, then insert it behind the same four threads, bringing it out two threads below the last thread. Draw the thread taut, bringing the fabric threads together. Continue along one side of the entire border.

To form the ladder rungs for ladder hemstitch, repeat the same process on the other side of the border, gathering together the same threads groups.

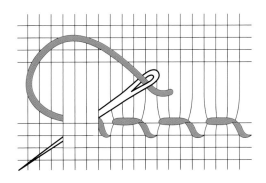

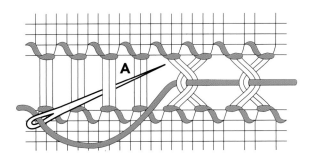

Interlaced Hemstitch

For this delicate border stitch, first work a ladder hemstitch. Then fasten a long thread at the right-hand side of your border. Pass your needle across the front of two groups of threads (ladder rungs) and then insert it from left to right under the second group, at A. Now insert the needle under the first group from right to left (B)—this twists the second group (rung) over the first group. Pull the thread through firmly so that it lies in the center of the twisted groups. Repeat with the next two thread groups (rungs).

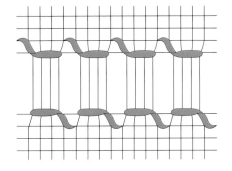

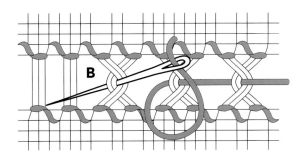

Stitches

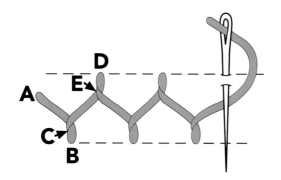

Open Cretan Stitch
(Flannel Stitch)

For this border stitch, bring the thread to the right side of your work at A, insert it at B and bring it back up at C. For the next stitch, insert the needle at D and bring it up at E. Space your stitches over an equal number of threads; all stitches lie at right angles to the imaginary guiding lines shown in the drawing.

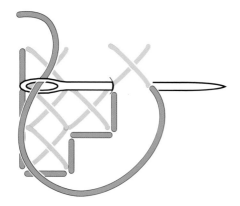

Outline Stitch

This useful and basic stitch, also called the back stitch, works for any outlining called for in the book. Bring your needle up on the right side of your work, just to the right of the figure you want to outline. Take a small stitch backward, then bring the needle up again in front of the first stitch, a stitch-length away. As you work around the figure, insert your needle each time at the end of the previous stitch.

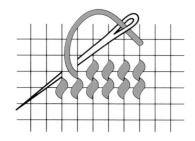

Petit Point Stitch

The most common canvas stitch, petit point's small diagonal stitches, which are formed like half a cross-stitch, should always lie in the same direction.

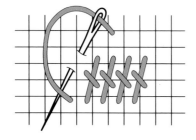

Rumanian Stitch

For this elongated cross-stitch, also called a knotted stitch, make a long slanted stitch, as shown in the drawing, then tie it down with a short, diagonal stitch across its center; bring your needle up for the second full stitch directly beside the beginning of the first, for a tight row of stitches.

Stitches

Running Stitch

To make this simple stitch, push the needle up and down through the fabric, crossing the same number of threads with each stitch.

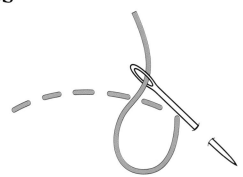

Satin Stitch

Often used for filling in flower centers, mouths, and other areas that need solid color, these flat, even stitches completely cover the fabric. On the right side of your work, bring the needle up at one edge of the area you want to cover and insert the needle directly across the area from that entry point. Make each stitch right beside the previous one, allowing no fabric to show through.

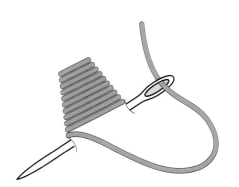

Star Stitch

To make this decorative stitch, bring your needle down at the center of the star, up at the outer end of a ray, and then back down at the center; repeat for each ray.

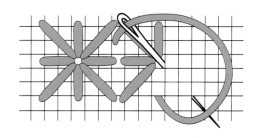

Stem Stitch

A popular stitch for outlining, stem stitches often appear in samplers for working the stems of flowers and leaves. Bring the needle up to the right side of your work along a marked or imaginary line on your fabric, insert it just to the right of the line, and bring it back up half a stitch-length back. As you work along the line, insert your needle each time at the end of the previous stitch for a continuous, braided look.

SPECIAL THANKS

to Shirley Turner of Cross Stitch Corner / Corner Frame Shop, 856 Merrimon Avenue, Asheville, North Carolina, for technical advice and for the loan of some of the materials pictured on pages 8–9 and on the endpapers.

SOME OF THE QUOTATIONS FROM
EARLY AMERICAN SAMPLERS
WERE DRAWN FROM:

Samplers: Five Centuries of a Gentle Craft, by Anne Sebba (New York: Thames and Hudson, 1979);

The Sampler Book, by Irmgard Gierl (Asheville, N.C.: Lark Books, 1984);

Historic Samplers, by Patricia Ryan and Allen D. Bragdon (Boston: Little, Brown, 1992); and

Samplers & Samplermakers: An American Schoolgirl Art, 1700–1850, by Mary Jaene Edmonds (New York: Rizzoli, 1991).

INDEX